Praise for *The Sun Is Up*

"Sleeper, awake," Paul sings, "and the light of Christ will shine on you." In these personal reflections, Martha tells the story of how she, like Paul, has woken up and had the scales fall from her eyes. In a church culture that loves its willful blindness, this memoir comes from a powerful white lady who has seen the light, and now has an important song to sing.

—Greg Jarrell
Author of *A Riff of Love: Notes on Community and Belonging*
Founder of QC Family Tree

For anyone who wants to do the real work of racial reconciliation, this book is a true, if bracing, gift. Kearse raises up, in searingly honest and often achingly painful ways, the unintentional and unknowing ways in which we often trip ourselves up and the harm we often do to others in the process. She brings a mature faithfulness as a reader of the Bible, a deep grasp of good theology and its comforts and demands, and a fierce love for people, churches, and the Church. Writing not as an outside critic but as a passionate insider willing to share the ways in which she has been "blind, asleep, and useless," Kearse also gives witness to the possibility of personal transformation that renders us capable of becoming part of God's transforming work.

—Rev./Rvda. LeDayne McLeese Polaski
Executive Director/Directora Ejecutiva
BPFNA ~ Bautistas por la Paz

Smyth & Helwys Publishing, Inc.
6316 Peake Road
Macon, Georgia 31210-3960
1-800-747-3016
©2018 by Martha Dixon Kearse
All rights reserved.

*All of the author's proceeds from the sale of this book will be donated to
two organizations currently working on racial justice:
QC Family Tree, in Charlotte, North Carolina, and
The Listening—specifically their Freedom School Project—in Lynchburg, Virginia*

Library of Congress Cataloging-in-Publication Data

Names: Kearse, Martha Dixon, author.
Title: The sun is up : one minister's awakening to racial reconciliation / by
Martha Dixon Kearse.
Description: Macon, GA : Smyth & Helwys Publishing, [2018] | Includes
bibliographical references.
Identifiers: LCCN 2018019616 | ISBN 9781641730617 (pbk. : alk. paper)
Subjects: LCSH: Reconciliation--Religious aspects--Christianity. | Race
relations--Religious aspects--Christianity. | United States--Race
relations.
Classification: LCC BT734.2 .K37 2018 | DDC 277.3/083089--dc23
LC record available at https://lccn.loc.gov/2018019616

Martha Dixon Kearse

THE SUN IS UP

One Minister's Awakening to Racial Reconciliation

This book is dedicated to the people of
St. John's Baptist Church in Charlotte, North Carolina,
and to my family:
Tim, Barbara, Deanna, Dave; Monty, Mattie, Conner, Anna;
Henry, Anna Lynn; Debora, Rep, Akur, Aluel.

Acknowledgments

The author wishes to acknowledge, with much gratitude, the following organizations:

St. John's Baptist Church in Charlotte, North Carolina

The M. Christopher White School of Divinity
at Gardner-Webb University

Friendship Missionary Baptist Church
in Charlotte, North Carolina

The Baptist Peace Fellowship
of North America/Bautistas por la Paz

Mecklenburg Ministries

Raising South Sudan and Mothering Across Continents

The South Sudanese Community of Charlotte

and the following individuals for reading and
providing feedback on this book:

LeDayne Polaski (Executive Director, BPFNA/BPLP)
Dr. Steve Harmon
Dr. Becky Shenton
Dr. Tim Dixon (Dad)
Mrs. Barbara Dixon (Mom)

Contents

Where shall I go from your Spirit?
    Or where shall I flee from your presence?
If I ascend to heaven, you are there!
    If I make my bed in Sheol, you are there!
If I take the wings of the morning
    and dwell in the uttermost parts of the sea,
even there your hand shall lead me,
    and your right hand shall hold me.
If I say, "Surely the darkness shall cover me,
    and the light about me be night,"
even the darkness is not dark to you;
    the night is bright as the day,
    for darkness is as light with you.

Psalm 139:7-12 (ESV)

Introduction

When you are arm in arm with your fellow clergy in the middle of a protest march that has, shall we say, turned a corner, and a lovely, small woman in nice clothes next to you asks, "Why are you here?" it can be difficult to answer the question. The pitch-black sky is just background for the blaring lights of Charlotte's Epicenter, usually a bustling, happy place. At that moment, your face is inches from a line of policemen, two deep, each of whom is dressed in full riot gear with his hand on some sort of automatic rubber bullet or pellet gun that he holds across his chest. You are aware that there are children in the crowd behind you—elementary school-aged and younger, as well as those who look like adults and are actually still children. You have linked arms with the other clergy who are there: a white man in a suit next to you, next to him a young white woman, next to her a tall black man in a suit, and on down the line. Things have gone precipitously south in this march. Emotions are running high. You are not even sure who in your church knows you are here; you take a brief moment to think about who will see your face on the televised news or in a newspaper and take offense. That has happened before. Still, you know the real answer to why you are here, and you tell the woman, "We are clergy. We were asked to be here." She accepts that answer and turns, once again, unarmed and still in her office clothes, to face the police.

In 2016, as the events in Charlotte, North Carolina, around the shooting of Keith Lamont Scott began to unfold, I was just starting the project stage of my doctoral work at Gardner-Webb University's

M. Christopher White School of Divinity. I had chosen the topic of the theology of hospitality in the Bible and its message to us about racial reconciliation. I had attended one meeting of the group of people who had agreed to be in my doctoral study, consisting of members from my own church, St. John's Baptist in Charlotte, and members from a sister church, Friendship Missionary Baptist in Charlotte (a predominantly black church). The project was the culmination of thirty years of my trying to figure out what I might do to help build peaceful relationships between white people and black people, observing myself to have failed. The events in Charlotte that happened after a police officer shot Mr. Scott served to reinforce the lessons I have been learning, and I hope to share those lessons with you in this book.

The Work

In recent years, as it has become more apparent to me exactly what my work in racial reconciliation might be, I have come to realize two things: that my primary work is with other white people—to help them to hear the message of what I have learned—and that it probably will take a book to cover what I need to say. Let's be up front about the very ugly, very large elephant in the room: many white people have been resistant to the real work of racial reconciliation. As a group, white Christians are particularly egregious in their resistance for several reasons, most of which are cultural:

1. In order to do the work of racial reconciliation, white people have to participate in uncomfortable conversations, some of which are confrontational, and many don't like to be either uncomfortable or confrontational.

2. White people are tuned in to their own rights. They will not willingly hold blame that they do not think is truly theirs to hold. Because of this, the conversation typically ends when individual white people feel that they are being blamed for slavery, for the Jim Crow, or for other events in the past over which they had no control.[1]

3. White people believe their systems—educational, judicial, employment, and housing—to be fair. When black people tell them

about police violence against black people or about bias in the justice and educational systems, white people don't believe them. Whites trust their systems over the words of black brothers and sisters.

4. White people, particularly white Christians, do not like change.

My personal experience of church—an institution with which I have had much experience—has been that church people would rather live for years with the roof literally falling in over their heads than have the difficult conversation about how to fix the roof. One thing I have learned over the course of my career is that *nothing happens until you have the tough conversation.* Delay it, do it halfway, ignore it—however we avoid it, the truth is that progress is stymied until the people in the system (in this case, the church) are willing to confront the real issues in hard, sincere, painful, revealing, and honest conversation. Only then can any action occur; only then will the actions that are taken begin to move the system forward.

Why Me?

The reason I bear some responsibility for talking to white people, and to white Christians in particular, is that I am one of you. I am, head to toe, legitimate. Born to Baptist ministers, raised as a PK (Preacher's Kid) in the home of Baptists until I joined the BSU (Baptist Student Union) at college and then the ranks of Baptists jilted by the Southern Baptist Convention, I was middle-aged before I heard a call to ministry, which I answered in 2001. I spent five and a half years getting a Master of Divinity (MDiv) and then three more getting a Doctor of Ministry (DMin), and I have been in ministry for sixteen years at St. John's Baptist Church in Charlotte. And, like the apostle Paul, I know that counts for *skubalon,*[2] except in this one reality: I am one of you. I am your child and the creation of your culture. You can choose whether or not to listen to what I say here. What you cannot say is that I am some outsider, some interloper or troublemaker. Baptists (and I include Southern Baptists in this title) cannot deny that I am theirs, any more than the College of William & Mary, Gardner-Webb University's M. Christopher White School of Divinity, the cities of Crozet, Richmond, Lynchburg, and Charlotte, or my husband and children can deny that I am theirs. You can disagree with me, but much of what I hope to share are things that are not a matter of opinion but rather of experience. This book describes my experiences as I experienced them. You may feel free to disagree with my conclusions, but my experiences of these events are my own.

Good Theology

In 2016–2017, I completed my doctoral project for a doctorate in ministry at Gardner-Webb. My project involved studying the theology of hospitality and applying that theology to the work of racial reconciliation. In this book, the theology of hospitality (which is only partly about having casseroles ready when guests show up and very much about safety, welcome, preparedness, and personal risk) will be at the center of what I hope to share. As always, people use the Bible for many things, and one of the most common uses is to prove something that they want to be true. The way to guard against that temptation and to truly listen to the message of the Bible is by using good theology. In this book, I will define good theology as

1. a theology based on pervasive themes of the Bible (in other words, I can find multiple instances in the Bible where the theology appears, and it is applied in many different circumstances);

2. a theology that holds up to the experience of the church in history—all of the church, not just the white or European/American one;

3. a theology in keeping with common sense, in keeping with the human experience we have had over the millennia and that we are having now;

4. and a theology in keeping with my experience of God. I cannot speak to anyone else's experience of God and won't attempt to do so.

The Bible was used to justify slavery. It is currently being used to vilify and condemn people for loving others in ways some people do not like. It is used to talk about "family values" and to justify an often destructive obsession with nationality.[2] By the time this book reaches your hands, it will have passed through the hands of several people I respect who are more learned than I will ever be on theology. In submitting this writing to other readers before it gets to you, it is my hope that, while it may not reflect a theology with which every person agrees, it is a theology presented with intellectual, academic, spiritual, and personal integrity.

The theology of hospitality is pervasive in the Bible. In my work, I counted more than 140 separate instances in which the theology of offering hospitality to outsiders is invoked. It appears in books of law (Lev 19:33-34), books of poetry (Job 29:14-16 and Ps 39:12-13), books of prophecy (Jer 7:5-7), Gospels (Matthew 25), and epistles (Eph 2:11-22 and Heb 13:2). In these texts and others, we are told about God's hospitality to us, offering us a place in a world that belongs entirely to God. We are told to remember that we have been strangers and outsiders, and so we should remember those times when we meet a stranger. We are told that, just as God protects us, we should offer protection to the stranger, placing their needs above our own. We are told that, not having the perspective of God, we would do well to make sure that we offer our best hospitality to anyone who crosses our threshold, as the "least of these" are, in fact, the same as our Lord Jesus Christ (Matt 25:40).

Lessons Learned

This is a book about what I have learned. In the first section, each chapter will conclude with the lessons I have learned as I understand them. Necessarily, this narrative will contain the mistakes I have made along the way. I do not present those mistakes as being anyone's other than mine. It is not my position that I have been particularly forward thinking or morally superior in any way in my actions. In fact, part of this book will contain my apology for the ways I have been blind, asleep, and useless in the work of making right what is egregiously wrong in our culture. I am neither a leader in the movement toward justice nor particularly notable for my actions. What I can do is bear witness and teach. What I can do is confront my own privilege—the many ways in which I have had advantages, whether I recognized them as such or not—honestly and share the work I have had to do (and still have to do) to keep that privilege at bay. It is my hope that, in reading my narrative, you might be able to step back and observe your own.

Challenge

The second part of this book contains some words of challenge. I do not know what work you might have to do toward racial reconciliation. In my experience, this work takes many different forms. What I can say for sure is that if you are a white person in America, and particularly if you identify yourself as a Christian white person, you do have work to do. If you are a Christian person in America—white, black, or any other shade of flesh—you have work to do. In reading this book, perhaps other people might be able to say to themselves, "If she can do something, I can, too."

When my son was still small (he is 6'5" now), he was an early riser—a very early riser. He would come into our room, where his father and I were sleeping on a bed that put us right at eye level with him. He would lean his face into mine (in a way that would have been both terrifying and creepy had he not been two years old), and he would wait quietly until I opened my eyes. When I startled awake and recovered from the shock of having a face so close to mine, he would say, "The sun is up." What he meant was, "It is way past time for you to be up and fixing me some breakfast, preferably something with sugar and bacon."

This is our challenge. The sun is up. It is long past up. We have known that we have work to do and have avoided it for a long time. And, even if hearing about it in this way is startling, it doesn't change the fact that it is time for us to act. The time for sleep is over. The sun is, most decidedly, up.

The Very Good News

Some parts of this book may be hard to read. It's painful to think that we have been hurting people. I genuinely believe that most white Americans do not want their actions (and inactions) to hurt anyone and that they perceive that their systems are in everyone's best interest. The last chapter of this book (before the resources section) is about the other side of this work: the reward. Read it first if you want. Read it again between every chapter if you want. Remind yourself that there is a world where we are not divided by culture or race or gender. It does exist, and there is a model for it in the New Testament. This, right now, right here, is the kingdom of God—the banquet is going on today, and we can be a part of it. Sitting down to a table with everyone, with anyone, is the very definition of the kingdom of heaven. And freeing ourselves from our anger and our frustration and our sense that something is wrong is one of the best things we can do for ourselves. Go bravely—and offer yourself grace along the way.

Words of Encouragement

I have heard from white people, again and again, this sentence: "I am so tired of being blamed for racism. I don't want to talk about how I am the bad guy anymore." Here are the best words of comfort I can offer you:

1. Everyone has to deal with his or her prejudices. This is absolutely, 100 percent true for every human on the planet.
2. You do not have to answer for anyone else's prejudices, racisms, or behaviors.
3. You are responsible for what you actually do, what you actually believe, and what you actually benefit from. All you are being asked to do is your part, and you do have a part.

The truth, though, is that the lights are on, the sun is out, and we can't pretend we do not know that we have work to do. This book is my attempt to share the work I have done, the work I am still doing, and the ways I need to repent. If you get weary while you are reading this, put it down. Go have a sandwich. Take a walk. Talk to your friends. Have a cookie. And then pick it back up and keep reading. Keep working. I believe that facing these lessons is part of our work as followers of Jesus Christ, and self-pity is not something our faith encourages. Be strong and courageous. Think about how wonderful it is going to be when this work is done and we can be free of it at last.

Notes

1. Jim Crow laws refer to laws created in the early twentieth century to prevent black Americans from voting and to keep their living, work, and public lives separate from white Americans.

2. *Skubalon* is Greek for "dung" or "garbage."

3. Loving the country of your birth and giving your government *carte blanche* to do whatever it wants are two entirely different things.

The Lessons

You've got to be taught to hate and fear
You've got to be taught from year to year
It's got to be drummed in your dear little ear
You've got to be carefully taught.

—"You've Got to be Carefully Taught,"
Richard Rodgers and Oscar Hammerstein II, *South Pacific*

Carefully Taught

When you start listening to the stories of people's experiences of growing up, as I did over the last two years, it is impossible to miss that cultural identity in our country is both bred and nurtured into us. In the course of my doctoral project, I collected the stories of people who grew up in church, all of whom would be identified professionally as "white-collar" workers. About half were white and half were black,[1] and the group was about half male and half female. In the stories of most of the white people, there were two common threads:

1. As they grew up, their experience of black people was limited—possibly completely limited to one nice black lady who cleaned their house or cared for them when they were children.

2. Unless they grew up in a household with an overtly racist parent (which was the exception in my research rather than the rule), white people neither talked about nor thought about race on any regular basis until their teenage years.

The stories of the black people I interviewed also had some commonalities:

1. As they grew up, their experience of white people was very limited.

2. Many experienced segregated schools as vastly superior to integrated schools, In the segregated schools, their black teachers

pushed them and took them seriously and saw them as people, while the white teachers in the integrated schools ignored them or treated them as if they could not learn.

3. Not a day went by in their childhoods when they were not aware of their own race. Most were encouraged to keep their heads down, work hard, and not make trouble. Most were made aware that they could not count on the systems of the city, county, state, or country in which they lived to protect them from harm.

Pretty Standard, Really

My own experience was, sadly, not unique. I was born in 1963, the day before Dr. Martin Luther King, Jr., gave his speech on the steps of the Lincoln Memorial. As much as she is an admirer of Dr. King, my mother tells me that she did not watch the speech as she was recovering from the delivery of her second daughter in the hospital in the way they did things back in the sixties, which was to treat women giving birth as if they were both ill and unclean.[2] For the first five years of my life, I lived in Yancey Mills, a neighborhood outside of Crozet, Virginia, which is a small town outside of Charlottesville. For me, it was idyllic; we lived in a parsonage just across the street from the church where my father was a minister. We spent our days visiting church members in the neighborhood, having tea parties, playing in the churchyard, and enjoying those lovely, long days before school started. The mountains of Virginia, which, as we all know, are where God lives, still feel like home to me.

When I was five, we moved to Richmond, technically to Chesterfield County. My father's parents lived there, and when we moved into our little ranch house in the suburbs, my grandmother offered to pay the wages of a nice lady named Mary who would come clean our house periodically. In my memory, she is the first black person I ever knew. She did not interact with us; my mother was not much for having someone else clean her house (except her children—she was fine with that), and I think Mary's tenure with us was short lived. Life in Richmond was harder for me than life in Charlottesville, mostly because I was expected to go to school. In 1968, no one knew anything about ADHD or learning disabilities. Wise woman that she was, my mother knew that I would be unhappy at home when my older sister, Deanna, was at school, but she and my father both remained flummoxed at the fact that I did not take to school the way my sister had. In the sixties and seventies, great minds had turned their attention to the educational system, and their idea of what elementary school students needed was to be gathered into one huge room and given free reign while being expected to complete assignments. For me, this overstimulation was as nightmarish as the endless nothingness of activity that was naptime.

Despite being shoved in with every kindergartener in the county, I did not encounter a black child in school. Richmond schools were on a city/county system—children in the city went to separate schools from children in the county, which helped that old city (and many others) bypass segregation quite neatly. In June 1969, my sister died from Reye's Syndrome, a complication of chicken pox (which each of us in my family got multiple times). She died suddenly, within a matter of days, as her fever rose and doctors at that time had no way to save her from the damage it was doing to her brain. I was not quite six years old, and my brother was two and a half when we learned the lesson of life that some people don't have to face until well into adulthood: bad things can happen to you. I do not tell you the story of the death of my sister to imply that it made me a better person, or that somehow it gave me insights that other people don't have. For me and for my brother, it was horrible. Deanna was my north star—the person by which I guided my entire life. She came to be with me in the kindergarten class when I had trouble. She told me what to say when I didn't have words. Losing her has not added some poignant blessing to my life.

What her death might have done was to create a crack in my life of privilege. After her death, there was never a moment in which I believed that I was immune to the whims of the universe. My parents had little patience for the bad theologies of death. My mother rejects that Deanna was "an angel that God needed back" or that her death was God's will. My mother was a nurse; for her, Deanna's death was a fact of science—she was sick, and doctors did not know how to help her body heal. God was with my mother, particularly in the form of a lovely friend who called her every day and lovely church people who held her and my father close through those years and after. My parents understood their daughter's death to be a failure of science, a fact of nature, and a great and terrible loss. They taught me to believe the same.

I am not naturally risk averse. Had my sister lived, I would probably have been the child who jumped out of airplanes and off mountains with a few yards on nylon between myself and certain death. Deanna's death, though, meant that I could not casually risk my own life. The world was, in fact, much less safe than I had originally been led to believe. And, as a second child, not used to stepping boldly into new things, I had to learn to be a first child, a task I did exceptionally poorly. It was not until I had my own children that I understood what I was supposed to do as a first child—my own first child did it effortlessly. But I could not fulfill those tasks, and the combination of that loss and my ADHD made for several awkward and confusing years.

The Lovely Africans and Other Beautiful People

In Richmond, the Southern Baptist Convention had one of its stalwart institutions, the Foreign Mission Board (now called the International Mission Board). We often hosted visiting missionaries in our home, and in the early seventies we met a family from Nigeria who became our good friends. Michael and Christiana Aluko came to Richmond with their son, Shagum, and visited us often. Shagum was my brother's age, and they played happily together from the time we first knew them. I was about ten years old when Christiana gave birth to a daughter (whose name I never learned because they wait until children are two years old before naming them). During that same time, I began accompanying my mother and the WMU circle to their missions projects. They did a Bible school in a downtown church, and I remember being the only blonde in a room full of black children for those happy, if chaotic, VBS weeks. In addition, her circle went once a month to the girls' wing of the juvenile detention center in Richmond. I went with her just about every time, admiring those older girls, both black and white, and their cool, dorm-like rooms. I have a distinct memory of sitting with an older girl on one of those evenings and hearing her ask me what I wanted to do when I grew up. I said, "I want to come here."

In 1975, we moved to Lynchburg, Virginia, where I learned what it means to be an outsider. In Lynchburg, you must be a native, preferably of several generations' legitimacy, to be part of the inner circle. I was not. Neither was my brother. In Lynchburg, my brother and I came up against what we refer to as "The Children of the Corn": the most beautiful, meanest kids we'd ever encountered. Lynchburg taught us how to fight bullies, which we did with some regularity over the next few years. As a female, I mostly fought in my neighborhood and not in school, but there was one memorable occasion in my seventh-grade homeroom class. Lynchburg offered the first truly integrated classrooms I had experienced. For the first time, I went to school with white kids and black kids. One day in my classroom, a tall black boy was picking on a black girl. I don't remember what he was doing, but it bothered me enough that I intervened (I have always been nosy). I told him to leave her alone, at which point they both turned on me. I stood up and he pushed me down. This had all happened with the teacher out of the classroom. She returned just as I was standing up again and getting ready to push back. I remember being taken out in the hall with the black boy (the black girl, whom I was defending, was not included in this) and being fussed at for fighting.

I didn't get along with either the white kids or the black kids for that first year. I was an outsider, not welcomed by the white kids. Overly tall and awkward, nerdy and a teacher's pet, I was not an attractive friend to anyone. I was picked on by the tough girls in gym and targeted for games of dodge-ball and "prison." I was not welcomed by the black girls either, with this one exception: they loved my hair. For most of seventh grade, I served as a Barbie head for a small group of black girls. They did not talk to me but over me, to each other, while they brushed and braided my hair. I was simply glad to be acknowledged (not really as a human being, but at least with other human beings) and had no idea how to say "no" to their requests to do this, and so I served my time as plastic doll head while

I tried to think of one thing I could say that would make them like me. I did not succeed.

Eventually, a few white kids in Lynchburg took pity on me, notably the fabulous Ginny, who took me under her wing and attempted to teach me how to live in decent society, and Laurie, also an immigrant into the town, who just enjoyed chucking notes across the room and making Ginny crazy with me. I developed good friendships in the band and at church. I rose as high as one can get in band circles: I became the drum major my senior year. I never cracked the code of Lynchburg society—not that I really tried—and I never figured out how to be true friends with the black girls. Laurie was (and is) an athlete and had many good friends, black and white, among her teammates; I never found a way in beyond friendly acquaintance. Despite the fact that I still did not know I had ADHD, I figured out some things about school and found that I was smart, at least in some classes (not math). I felt pretty good that I had conquered the awkwardness of my early adolescence and the failures of my elementary school academics; if I couldn't figure out how to bridge the race barrier, I guessed I could live with that.

In short, my growing-up years were fairly typical of a white, Christian person in America. My parents created a home that was respectful and loving to people of other races but did not question existing systems. This is not to say that my parents never questioned the systems, but they were adults, and they did not talk about such things with me. Their home was always welcoming, and their treatment of people was always kind. My father actually worked with his church and held the first combined service of worship between black and white Baptists in Lynchburg soon after his arrival in that city. They sought to work inside the systems as they existed at the time, in keeping with the experiences of most of the white people I have talked with in the last two years. As children, my brother and I heard racist talk, but not from our parents; it wasn't permitted in our home. If we went to schools segregated by location, it was because they were the "best" schools, not because they were segregated. We did not talk about race or think about what it meant to be white.

Our African friends, the Alukos, introduced some wonderful conversations about culture. My mother's favorite story about Michael is that one time, at dinner, they were talking about a mutual friend, Nancy Cousins, who had been in Kenya with missionary friends, when a chief of one of the villages took notice of her. Nancy had red hair, and the chief offered to buy her from the missionary, a transaction that the missionary declined. Wanting Nancy to know of his love for her, the chief placed a gift for her in the trunk of the missionary's car: a bush rat. When the white people at our family table heard this, the universal reaction was, "Ewww!" Michael, seeing their reaction, said, "Ah, but it is delicious!"

Most people with whom I have talked had a similar upbringing—not particularly angry or racist but working under the assumptions that the systems within which we lived—systems of education, financial well-being, justice, housing, and religion—were fair and kind and just, and that they worked the way they were supposed to work. We assumed that people who worked hard could get out of poverty if they wanted to, no matter their skin color. We assumed that people who were arrested had done something to be arrested for. We assumed that schools were schools, and that it didn't matter whether children went to segregated or desegregated schools, whether neighborhoods were lily white or whether children encountered children of different races under normal, regular circumstances that allowed them to see each other as human. We did not do any research or ask the black people we knew what their experiences were. I'm not sure they would have told us if we had, since they had no reason to think we would believe them. We were blind, and when you are blind, you do not know what you cannot see. You don't try to see. That is what it means to be blind.[3]

Like most of the white people I know, I thought of myself as a non-racist, good person. When I heard the song from the musical *South Pacific*, "You Have to be Carefully Taught," I thought that I had been taught good things, and I had. I was taught respect and kindness. I was taught to see people as people. I was taught to do what I can to make the world better. But I was also taught to believe in the established systems and in institutions. I was taught not to question authority figures but to believe that they knew what was best and were acting in everyone's best interest. I was taught silence and acceptance and thus raised with a profound blindness to injustice.

Lessons

• *The world is not actually very safe.*
• *There are lots of different people out there, and many of them don't necessarily think I am awesome.*
• *I get by with a little help from my friends.*

Notes

1. In this book I will use the terms "white" and "black" with no capitalization. They are equally inaccurate. I have never for one moment been white. I was, for a time in my late teens and twenties, able to achieve an attractive caramel brown, which went nicely with my blonde hair and blue eyes. Now I could best be described as "blotchy beige." And even my South Sudanese friends, whose amazing dark skin is the most beautiful color I've ever seen, are not black; they are dark chocolate brown, the kind that is good for your heart. "African American," my young friend Kadia has taught me, is a term that does not include people of color who do not trace their origins to Africa. With the terms "black" and "white," I figure it is best to be wrong all the way around.

2. Another issue for another book.

3. I have never been physically blind, so I want to be careful here. My reference to blindness is metaphorical, and not meant to imply anything about human beings who experience physical blindness. Metaphorical blindness is willful, and physical blindness is not. All metaphors break down at some point.

Actually, Love Is *Not* All You Need

In 1985, after graduating from the College of William and Mary with a BA in English and education, I accepted a job in Charlotte, North Carolina (a city I had never heard of or been to, but randomly chose when they interviewed at W&M), to teach high school. The philosophy of school systems at that time for first-year teachers seemed to be the following:

1. Give new teachers all of the lowest-performing classes. Fill their rolls with the students everyone else has refused to teach.
2. Don't tell them where any materials are.
3. Fill their first week of work with mindless workshops about where to put the trashcan.
4. Throw them to the wolves.

My classroom was a trailer outside of the high school that first year. I lived in what was then called "Griertown." I got a dog (a beagle named Bill the Dog) and somehow went to work every day. I am proudest of three things that happened that year:

Love

I learned to love my students. They were, to a person, difficult. They had been unloved by their schools their entire lives—black and white, they had been shifted aside and neglected. By the time they got to me, in the eleventh grade, they were angry, jaded, and lost. They came from every possible segment of Charlotte society. Some spent their mornings doing chores on their farms before they came to school; some came straight from public housing. And I struggled to get through every day with them. The black girls took offense at everything I said. The white boys and the black boys took advantage of all the gaps in my discipline (which were plentiful). The quiet ones (black and white) stayed quiet and the loud ones stayed loud. It was in my abject failure as a teacher and a human being that I discovered the power of God. By February, I hated my students, each and every one. And I wanted to quit. I called my mother to tell her that I was never setting foot inside that school again. And my mother reminded me that I had felt called to this work. And (argh) she was right. And God intervened. And, in the weeks that followed, I found that I loved them despite myself. I know with all of my heart that I was incapable of loving those students on my own. But God wasn't incapable of that love, and God shared it with me. That's the only way I can fathom how my feelings for them changed almost over-night. I can still picture many of their faces.

African-American Literature

I had an amazing professor at Bill & Mary named Dr. Joanne Braxton. In 1984 when I took her course, she was a new professor, full of energy and enthusiasm. She taught me about African-American literature and helped me to love and appreciate its beauty. In 1984, it was all new to me. I think we read *The Invisible Man* when I was in high school, but I wasn't taught anything about the trajectory of African-American literature, nothing about the richness of the female writers or the power of slave narratives or the beauty of the tall tales or the angry hurt behind them all.[1] Dr. Braxton taught me about Frances E. W. Harper and Paul Laurence Dunbar and Countee Cullen and Richard Wright and Gwendolyn Brooks and Alice Walker and my great love Toni Morrison. In 1986, after talking to my mother on the phone, I decided to spend a month reading African-American literature with my students. We covered as many writers as we could; I practically broke the Xerox machine making copies (as none of these authors were represented in the official text that I eventually found in a locked and dusty back room). The white kids questioned the need to read these authors, and the black kids said little about it, but I felt better. I felt like I had done something important. And, if nothing else, it was different. I can't say that it made the kids respect or love me, but it was at least interesting, led to interesting conversations, and gave the students a reason to tolerate me.

Fred

At no time during the entire school year of 1985–1986 was Fred in danger of passing my class. Fred was one of those children who is doomed by his own intelligence. He was smart but probably dealing with a learning disability and certainly dealing with educational neglect. He was about my height (six feet) and dark-skinned with a beautiful face and angry, angry eyes. He was full of mischief and, when he was in class, mostly good-natured (or asleep). He failed to turn in just about every assignment I gave. I had no way to pass him, as pretty much all his grades were zero. But in May, I decided to do our last unit on American theater, dividing the classes into groups and having them learn and perform one scene from a classic American play. Fred's group was doing *Death of a Salesman*. Over that last month, they were to choose a scene, assign roles, design a set and paint it, memorize their lines, and practice their piece. On the day they performed, Fred offered one of the most convincing, amazing, and powerful performances of the part of Willy Loman I have ever seen. He was better than Dustin Hoffman.[2] I can still hear him scream, "I am Willy Loman and you are Biff Loman!"[3] We all forgot, for a few moments, that he was Fred. While I was not able to help Fred pass eleventh grade English after struggling to either control or teach him all year, I was able to offer him one moment to shine. What I think about, often, is how much that moment seemed to matter and also how little it changed the trajectory of his life.

My Part of the Solution

And so that, I thought, was my part in the solution to racial issues. I would love my students. I found a way to do that. I would teach African-American literature—a lot of African-American literature. I would try to find ways to engage my students and offer them the attention they had been denied for a long time. When I started teaching at this high school, there were 2,400 students in three grades. Each day, we reenacted the entropy that is inherent in the universe, and each day I went home to Bill the Dog, thinking I was doing good work. And I think I was. I think it's important here to note that while I still had much to learn (as do many, many white people), some of the things I did were helpful. In 1986, when parents first started making noise about going back to neighborhood schools, I spoke at the school board meeting with a bunch of other teachers and students in defense of busing. I still have my button that we made, which says, "Busing Is Working."

In the 1980s, this public high school was a beautiful, chaotic place. It housed the most eclectic collection of human beings to which I have ever belonged. There, I braved the cancerous fumes of the teacher's lounge (everyone smoked in Charlotte in 1985—even the students had a "smoking patio") to listen to the conversations of Baker Hood (white) and Roosevelt Washington (black) about history and culture. I valued the stern advice of Mrs. Amos (a tiny black teacher who could control large groups of students with a single, laser-like glare and whose first name I still do not know) and felt thrilled if she offered me any praise. I marveled at the way Betty Holland (white) did her job as guidance counselor with such fierce determination and grace. The school was filled with brilliant teachers—black, white, gay, straight, atheist, Jewish, Christian, you name it. Being there opened my eyes to the loveliness of diversity and to the wild and chaotic nature of freedom.

I moved to another school in 1989—a school further out in the suburbs. It was a new public high school and could not have been more of a polar opposite to the first high school in its culture. If the god of the first was "Freedom," the god of the second was "Achievement." At that time, schools in Charlotte-Mecklenburg were required to maintain a balance of the black/white student population. While the teachers and administration of the second school showed no signs of overt racism, it quickly became clear that anyone or anything that stood in the way of their being the number-one school in the system was not welcome there. During that first year, I began to hear from my black students that the police were pulling them over when they came to school functions. It was the first time I heard of being pulled over for "driving while black." Students began to tell me that some adults talked to them about applying to move to a school where they would be "more comfortable" or "closer to home." Black students who contributed to the success of the school were welcomed most: exceptional athletes were offered extra tutoring and treated as high school royalty by faculty and staff. This was not true, however, of exceptional artists or exceptional band members or exceptional actors. Students who were not exceptional but who caused no problems were accepted; any students who caused disruptions were encouraged to go elsewhere. By the time I left this high school in the late nineties, it was an almost entirely white school.

At first, I tried to help by joining the National Association for the Advancement of Colored People (NAACP). I did so in response to a growing sense that black students were struggling in that environment; I joined with the hope that I would be able to offer some support to the students. This was the first time I began to sense that I was not welcome because I was white.[4] By that time, I had been in enough rooms where I was the odd man out to know when I wasn't truly welcomed as part of the group. I didn't understand it at the time, but I didn't resent it. I didn't know what my presence could do anyway, and if I wasn't wanted there, I figured I wouldn't come. The truth is that while I might have complained about the treatment of black students to other teachers, and while I might have railed about it at home, I risked nothing. I said nothing that mattered, nor did I do anything that helped even a single student stand up against a system that was actively working against them. This was long before I began to have real conversations about race with black peers who felt that they could be honest with me. There were so many lovely, intelligent black educators in my world, and I remember how they looked at me. I think they believed that I had good intentions, but they saw my ignorance and my blindness. They doubted my willingness to do anything that mattered. It is perhaps true that, at that time, they themselves did not know what to ask of me. What could I do, anyway? If there is anyone lower in the power hierarchy in a high school (particularly one as focused on sports as this school was) than a fourth-year English teacher, I am not sure who it would be.

I made something of a sport of questioning my principal at staff meetings. He knew who I was—but just barely. And nothing I said made one iota of difference in his agenda. The school's administration set out to make this school the number-one school in Charlotte, something they achieved quickly. The principal there taught me the value of discipline and the power of presence, insisting that teachers stand at the doors while students changed classes, himself roaming the hallways like a rancher protecting the herd from the threat of wild cattle rustlers. I learned a great deal while I was there—values that the first high school could not teach me. Things like the power of planning, the relationship between discipline and safety, and how to throw up outside a trailer and return to class as if nothing had happened (I was pregnant twice while there).

I also learned a great deal about privilege. At this high school, I began to have administrators show up at my door with students trailing behind them. "Ms. Dixon," they would say (later Ms. Kearse), "Johnny here has been kicked out of Ms. _____'s class. She has said she will no longer teach him." I had not known this was an option in public school! I tended to just teach the students I was given. Apparently, the veteran teachers had something like a fantasy student draft, and there were quite a few students rejected from other classes who ended up in my wandering classrooms. I still couldn't figure out how to get students who never did any work to pass my class. Over the years, though, three things happened. First, I stopped using the textbook. At the beginning of the year, I would hand out the books, have students write their names in them, and instruct them to carefully secure the books in their lockers, where they should still be in June, when I would again take them up—hopefully in the exact same condition as they were given, as they had not been touched. I taught what I wanted to teach—I taught more writing, more nonfiction, more research. I asked students to choose their own books, and I gave reading time in class. I read aloud to them and tried getting them to do handwork (making quilt squares, learning to knit, etc.) while they were read to.[5]

Second, I stopped assigning homework in classes for students who were not planning to go to college. In the few classes I was given with college-bound students, I gave homework, because this was their lot in life. Having signed up to go to college, they would need to be in the habit of doing work on their own. My other classes, with "regular" students (as they were called at the time), had varying situations at home. One student I had (whom I still encounter from time to time) was pregnant at the same time I was pregnant with my first child. It didn't make sense to send kids like her home with work for which they might have no place, or time, to do it. So we wrote in class. We read in class. I decided that if we did it in class, I could make sure that they actually got a chance to do it.

Third and finally, we left the building. I picked random field trips. I didn't really care where we went; I just wanted to get my students out of that square brick of a building. We sold candy bars and raised our own money. My principal told me that if I took them out of the building I should expect to have to call law enforcement to deal with them. One memorable trip was to the Biltmore House, a place that holds no interest for me but was the one place from which I could get permission to take the students outside the city of Charlotte. On the way there, one student (white) told me that he had not been on a field trip during school hours since he was in the fourth grade. And I didn't have a single discipline problem on the whole trip. They wandered around that ridiculous building, some enjoying the sights, some just enjoying being outside on a lovely April day. And I did not care about the lack of educational opportunities offered during the trip.

My perspective on my job changed drastically from when I had started as a teacher. When I began teaching, I thought I was teaching English literature and writing. By the time I stopped teaching, in 1997, I had decided that my main objectives were

• not to do any more damage than had already been done;

- help students communicate the things they needed to communicate, in speech and in writing;
- get them successfully through one of their graduation requirements;
- let them feel loved.

I could not have cared less about whether we covered the assigned text. Which meant that, when the writing was on the wall about end-of-course testing and what it would mean for education, I found the time to be ripe for me to walk away from teaching. I had two little lives at home to care for, not to mention a marriage and a house to maintain, and I had never found ways to change the system. I could defy it on my small scale; I could question it and rant about it. But I didn't seem to be able to nudge it at all, not in any direction that seemed to matter to me.

Despite my defiance, I still took few risks on behalf of justice. I still believed in the system. Despite all evidence to the contrary, I still did not see that children were being hurt by a system that actively worked against them. I still trusted the system to be ultimately fair and just, despite the fact that I had witnessed its injustices. The truth is that I put my own children first, and I didn't bother to look outside my own experience or attempt to step into a world that was not my own. If I thought about a solution at all, it involved leaving the system to continue to do what it would do, and saving only the children in my own sphere of influence. Like most white people, when it came right down to it, I punted.

Lessons

- *The system is failing a significant number of students.*
- *Inside the system, I am unable to do much to change those outcomes.*
- *Some people have more privilege than others. One of mine is that I can choose not to risk anything, really, and I can walk away.*

Notes

1. It's a pretty good guess that you weren't taught these things either. Start with Virginia Hamilton's amazing book *The People Could Fly*.

2. This is my opinion. Dustin, my apologies if you are offended.

3. Arthur Miller, *Death of a Salesman* (New York: Penguin Books, 1976).

4. More on this when we get to churches.

5. I am a huge proponent of the "no homework at any age" movement. Eight hours is more than enough time to spend on academic learning in any given day.

3

Guess Who's Coming to Dinner

In 2001 I became a minister—not something I had planned to do. In fact, about a year prior to this epic move, people in my church (where I was a deacon and directed an elementary-aged children's choir) began saying to me, "You should apply to be our children's minister." I laughed heartily. I knew what the life of a minister was like. I had paid attention to the man behind the curtain. I knew about vacations ending early, and late-night meetings, and the frustrations of 300 bosses, and the 365/24/7 nature of the job. No, thank you! But God's sense of humor is ever present, and so I was called. When I finally answered, it was kind of like putting on a well-worn sweater—it felt right. I loved my clergy badge and the fact that people stopped me in the hospital to ask me to pray with them. One man in an elevator at a Charlotte hospital said, "You don't look like any clergy I ever saw."

The Lost Boys of South Sudan

The year 2001 also saw the introduction of a group of the "Lost Boys from Sudan," into Charlotte, North Carolina. When a civil war in Sudan tore the country apart (1980s–2005), soldiers on both sides killed and maimed boys to prevent them from becoming soldiers. As a result, as many as 40,000 unaccompanied boys fled, traveling thousands of miles looking for safety. Of those who survived the journey, many ended up a large refugee camp in Kenya. Years later, the United States accepted some of the Sudanese refugees, and forty of these young men were relocated to Charlotte.[1]

When the people of St. John's Baptist were introduced to these young men, who were, at that time, truly lost in a world where novelties like refrigerator doors needed to be closed and there was a different soap for everything, they fell head over heels in love. I mean it: the people of St. John's loved (and continue to love) our South Sudanese brothers and sisters. And no one expected the ways in which these young men and then their wives and children would change our lives. Over our first two years with them, we taught them how to shop, how to drive (harrowing), how to write checks and pay taxes (only slightly less harrowing), how to navigate the American legal system and the American credit system, how to cook, and how to deal with winter.[2]

The thing is, we were white people. We were used to a system where we had knowledge, and we shared it. We had stuff, and we shared it. We spoke the native language, and we translated it. We were in power, and, from our top position, we could hand stuff down. What we weren't prepared for was what those guys gave to us. We didn't know what it would mean that they were ours forever. We didn't know what it would mean for them to invite us into their lives, to be part of funerals and weddings. We didn't know what it would mean to love their babies like our own and to be taken in among their people and welcomed as brothers and sisters. The thing is, South Sudanese people are proud and strong. They have been through a great deal, but they are very independent and didn't necessarily do what we wanted them to do or advised them to do.

For me, the big lesson came when I had the chance to go to South Sudan. Two of the Lost Boys, James Mijak and Ngor Magnol, had worked together with one of our church members, Phillips Bragg, and an organization named Mothering Across Continents, to build a school in Ruweng State in the northern part of South Sudan. There is little about this school that is not miraculous. When they raised the money and began to build there, there was no road for the trucks. There were no systems. There are no other buildings for miles. The school is, frankly, an impossible reality. Phillips had gone to see it in January, and I had a chance to go in June with Ngor and one of his mentors and sponsors, Karen Puckett. There is much to say about that trip, but here I simply want to focus on what I learned about race. South Sudan has been isolated for quite some time, primarily because of a constant state of war since the 1980s. For a short time after it became an independent state, money poured from oil companies wanting to capitalize on the natural resources of the country. That did not go well. When I visited in 2013, much of the progress had halted and parts of the area had fallen quickly into decay.

What I want to point out here is what it is like to be in a minority. In South Sudan, I was not just a minority—I was an oddity. I am six feet tall. I am blue-eyed. At first glance, even in the United States, some people think I am a man.[3] In South Sudan, white people are an oddity to begin with. There are international care workers, but they tend to be localized in certain areas of the country. Where I was, in Pariang, whites were pretty rare. Karen and I were the only ones I saw most of the time we were there.

The word "Denka," which is the name of the predominant tribe in South Sudan, means "people." The name for white people is "Kawaja," which I take to be somewhat pejorative based on the reactions of South Sudanese when I say it in reference to myself. At the very least, it means "outsider," but it seems also to have the connotation of "weirdo." Once, when we pulled up to a place where we hoped to have two minutes of Internet service in order to contact our families, we got out of the car where a group of children were playing. One little boy, about four years old, started dancing around in front of me. "Kawaja, Kawaja, Kawaja!" he said. Hot, tired, hungry, and offended, I struggled to find happy thoughts about this child. Another time, I went looking for water in the afternoon with Ngor. We were at a little stand, waiting our turn, when a young boy around ten years old walked up next to me. I looked down and watched him as he took in my shoes and my pants, and then raised his eyes to my face. "Kawaja!" he yelled, jumping back in horror. His friends laughed and comforted him. To him, apparently, I was something like the clown from the movie *IT*—white and terrifying.

Things Our South Sudanese Friends Have Taught Us

One of the tenets of faith at St. John's is that "From those to whom much is given, much is expected" (Luke 12:48). That is, out of our status of being okay, we give to others. We have no need of help of any kind—we are okay. We're so okay that the main thing we should be doing is giving to others. The South Sudanese, more than any other factor, have awakened me to the flawed and condescending nature of this philosophy. For one thing, it is terrible theology. At no point does the apostle Paul (who often talks about his many faults even while he tells people to be like him) or Jesus express that having become "okay," we should give to others. There is quite a bit about leaving other people's splinters alone and dealing with our own logs (Matt 7:3-5). And there is quite a bit about looking out for each other—but not because we have so much. In fact, Jesus pretty regularly asks those of us who have a lot:

- examine what we've got and look for the ways our wealth is causing us active harm (see the interpretation of the parable of the sower in Matt 13:22);
- let go of stuff (property), as well as rules, in favor of people (1 Tim 6:17);
- stop putting our faith in things of this world, which tend to fail (see the year 2008 and Matt 7:24-27).

The South Sudanese people accepted our help. But they also expected to help us.

I attended a Charlotte celebration of a South Sudanese couple's wedding that had already taken place elsewhere, and one of the women came to speak to me. I was sitting at the edge of the crowd, taking in all the dancing and happiness. Women at South Sudanese weddings, I should tell you, wear a special flowing garment over their clothes, which I did not have. This lovely woman, Theresa (who is always kind to me and often insists that I eat more of the food they have brought), took off her wrap and put it over my head. "Now, you are Sudanese!" she said. Never have I been with the South Sudanese when they have not welcomed me, cared for me, fed me, and honored me. Their gifts for hospitality are immense.

As we continued in our partnership with our South Sudanese friends, we began to understand something else: they were not always going to listen to us. South Sudanese people are proud, and they haven't always agreed with us about the choices they should make while living in America. Our priorities are not always theirs. And those of us who have stayed connected to them over the last sixteen years have a knowing smile we offer each other that says, "Yep, they're going to do what they're going to do!" South Sudanese people have been oppressed by war and tragedy, but they do not have a culture that tells them they are less important or less valuable than other people. They don't have the experience of white people as their oppressors, and they have no fear of us. They fought, and died, for the independence of their country, and white people never denied them the pride of that accomplishment. They have a defiant spirit that means they might make mistakes, but they make them on their own terms, and they do not give white people, in general, any special status.

The other realization I am coming to through these years of ministry is the growing sense that we—white Christians—are not actually okay. Despite our wealth and good fortune, the families of our church have suffered the same amount of depression, of dysfunction, of flawed family systems, of struggles with addiction or learning disabilities or left-handedness—you name it. We aren't okay. Not only that, but we aren't particularly good. Despite our "good intentions," we perpetuate flawed systems.

I read a sermon the other day from a former pastor at St. John's, Dr. Claude Broach. Dr. Broach is something of a legend at St. John's, and he was, by all accounts, an extraordinary individual. In 1974, he preached a prophetic sermon. He used the story from 1 Samuel 28—Saul and the Witch of Endor. Saul never listened to the good counsel he was getting from Samuel, and when he got himself into trouble, it was Samuel's voice he wanted to hear. Except in this instance, it was too late; Saul's chance to listen had come and gone. Dr. Broach preached a sermon called "Bring Up Samuel" in which he talked about the ways our culture refuses to listen to good counsel and continues to squander its chances for security. He talked about a "silly sort of optimism—the kind of optimism that refuses to look at things as they are," and he said that "we are tempted to a very silly sort of optimism about our country." He talked of how we abuse our land by squandering our resources and how we abuse our people with our foolish love for war. He said, "Can you see America at the door of the witch's cave, wanting her chance back again? Your children, your grandchildren, worried about energy, power, consumer goods, food? We had better get cured of our fatuous optimism." He talked about the people who attend church but who have given up any real faith in God. He called them "*yes, but* believers":

> Yes, but I don't intend to do anything about it . . . yes but, don't ask me for any money . . . yes, but don't put any moral restrictions on my selfishness . . . yes, but don't get religion mixed up with social reform or go meddling in race relations or war and peace or poverty and selfishness . . . .[4]

Dr. Broach saw all this in 1974, and somehow, we are still talking about the same issues today.

Civil Rights Tour of the South

In my own life, I kept being confronted with a growing body of information that said we had been willfully ignorant of egregious sins against humanity and still could not find a solution. Further information came in 2006, when I accompanied ten of my fellow MDiv students from Gardner-Webb on a journey through the southern states of Georgia and Alabama. Called "Civil Rights Tour of the South," the class was led by Dr. Sheri Adams, who told us that we would travel together to significant sites from the civil rights movement, sharing our thoughts with each other and then writing a paper on our experiences.

The students on this trip were about half white and half black.[5] We were about half female, half male, with some younger and some older students (like myself). Many of the ministers had been in ministry for several decades, and I was fortunate enough to get on the van with a bunch of the men. Our driver, Den (a white preacher who cooks like an angel), is one of the best storytellers I know, and he helped to keep the tone in the van light. When we stopped for dinner, Den often helped us pick the right place and the right dish. If the food was good, Den would say, "That right there—that's in the will of God." The black ministers gave each other endless joking abuse, and the slightest misspoken word might lead to half an hour of teasing from the group. Few experiences in my life have offered such highs juxtaposed to such lows. We stopped at civil rights museums in Atlanta, Montgomery, and Selma. Each was something like a Holocaust museum, leaving us in tears and stretched emotionally thin. Then, we would get back on the bus and laugh until we reached the next meal "in the will of God."

Martin Luther King, Jr.'s house in Montgomery feels like sacred ground. You can go up on the porch and put your fingers into the divot in the concrete where a bomb went off while his wife and baby girl were in the house. You can stand on the porch where he sent the people home who wanted to go fight in response to that bombing. In Montgomery, you can stand in silent awe at the beautiful stained-glass window in the back of the 16th Street Baptist Church, where four girls died from a bombing before Sunday school. You can be led through the Kelley Ingram Park by a homeless person, who will share with you the stories behind the powerful sculptures of dogs leaping out at you from both sides. In Selma, you can walk across the Edmund Pettis Bridge and picture what it must have been like to reach the top and see armed police and dogs on the other side.

The whole trip hurt. It hurt to see what the taxes of working Americans, both black and white, had paid for. Despite the fact that working black Americans paid taxes through all those years of Jim Crow and countless abuses, their systems and governments and neighbors actively worked against them to deprive them of everything from property and financial security to life and personal safety. One museum had a display of the robe of a member of the Ku Klux Klan. In the case with it was a book written by Franklin Dixon, maybe a membership guidebook. My maiden name is one I see on pencils from time to time, but it doesn't show up all that often. It hurt to see it on that book. I felt such shame and such sadness. How did I dare to feel solidarity with Rosa Parks when I had risked nothing in my life the way that she did when she received training, decided to act, and stepped onto a bus in her own town, knowing she would be arrested simply for sitting in the front of the bus? How blind was I to ask my black colleagues to be doing the work of racial reconciliation when most white people didn't even admit to the basic realities of the work?

At some point during the ride, I got into a conversation with one of the black ministers. He is about my age but has been in ministry his entire career. He is a person whose coloring is strikingly beautiful— he has dark, smooth skin, and his hair and beard are silver-white. Although he had enjoyed goofing around with the other ministers on the trip, he exuded a well-earned wisdom. We talked about worship and he said, "You know, we don't always follow the bulletin. If we have one hymn printed in the bulletin, but I feel the Spirit moving my heart to sing something, I just tell everyone to turn to a different hymn."

"Wow," I said. "That would never happen at my church."[6]

He said, "Well, white churches are better than we are about knowing the theology. You are better about preaching out of your education than we are. But we are better at listening to the Spirit."

"We could learn a lot from each other," I said.

"Yes," he said, "but neither of us are very good at that."

When we returned to Gardner-Webb, several of us shared our experiences in a chapel service for the divinity school. I shared my thoughts, my sorrow, my shame about finding my maiden name among the things of a KKK member. Afterward, many friends I had made among the black ministers spoke to me. They said, "You don't have to carry that. You are not a member of the KKK." Their words opened space in me and made me think seriously about one of the problems white people have in conversations about race: we feel great shame and sorrow, but those of us who are alive now did not actually own slaves. We may actively dislike racism and feel as powerless against it as black people do. This realization does not excuse us from the sins of which we are actually guilty. But acknowledging that we don't have to carry 400 years of oppression might make the conversation go better. We weren't even alive for most of those years. We must figure out what is actually ours to carry.

Lessons

- *Humans have a default setting of "othering," that is, defining people as substantially different from ourselves when their looks or practices make us uncomfortable. This natural safety response crosses all cultures. It serves us well when we are in danger and poorly when we are safe.*
- *White people tend to give/serve out of privilege—we expect thanks and even obedience. We are not very good at reciprocity and equality.*
- *The work of racial reconciliation involves bearing witness to many painful truths.*
- *The work of racial reconciliation involves listening.*
- *The work of racial reconciliation is deeply painful.*
- *Submitting oneself to the hard, painful work of racial reconciliation opens doors slowly.*
- *In order for white people to move forward in their part of racial reconciliation, we must find an accurate way to talk about what current, living white people are actually doing. We must practice listening to what our black friends and neighbors tell us. We must practice believing them.*

Notes

1. To learn more, see Norman Jameson, "Decades of life with the 'Lost Boys' from South Sudan: Charlotte church loves their neighbors as themselves," Baptist News Global, 8 April 2018. Available online at baptistnews.com/article/decades-of-life-with-the-lost-boys-from-south-sudan-charlotte-church-loves-their-neighbors-as-themselves/#.W32sCy3MyV5 (accessed 22 August 2018).

2. On one memorable occasion, the first winter they were in Charlotte, my friend Maggie Bond and I gathered up a bunch of donated winter items to take to the guys. When we pulled up to their apartment complex, they were all outside in the parking lot in T-shirts, shivering. We handed out the gloves, hats, scarves, and jackets and said, "Yeah, guys, bad news—you're probably going to have to hang out *inside* for a few months."

3. At a local Starbucks, I recently received my coffee with the name "Arthur" written on it.

4. Dr. Claude Broach, "Bring Up Samuel," sermon delivered at St. John's Baptist Church in Charlotte, NC, June 30, 1974.

5. Shameless plug: Gardner-Webb's Divinity School has one of the most diverse student bodies it has ever been my privilege to join. The faculty's attention to race has been intentional, and while they admit that there is still work to do, Gardner-Webb remains one of the few institutions I have attended as a student that has shown a real commitment to diversity.

6. And by never, I mean a situation of zero degrees Kelvin in hell.

4

Abject Failure

It is important to recognize that good people have been trying to do the work of racial reconciliation for years. In 1949, long before Jim Crow was gone from North Carolina, St. John's Baptist Church voted to open its doors to black Christians who might want to join. Under the guidance of pastor Dr. Claude Broach, the leadership of St. John's came to the decision to allow black members, and the church voted to do so.

The people of St. John's have always been somewhat defiant, especially in the face of outside forces telling them to whom they can and cannot offer membership. When Southern Baptists told them they could not let people join St. John's from other denominations without re-baptizing them, St. John's said, "Yeah, but we're going to do it anyway." When the North Carolina Baptist Association informed the church that they could either refuse to allow members who identified as lesbian, gay, bisexual, transgender, or queer (LGBTQ) or they would be removed from the association, St. John's said, "You keep your association. We don't play that game." St. John's has had female deacons for decades and female staff members since the 1960s. St. John's is the church about which I know the most, but it is not unique. Many, many houses of worship and people of faith have made progress in showing hospitality to everyone, and many have been intentional about trying to do the work of racial reconciliation. But Sunday morning worship is still known as what Martin Luther King, Jr., called the "most segregated hour of the week," and we need to consider why.

The Good Work

When I became a minister in 2001, I thought that at least part of my work would involve finding ways for white churches and black churches to join forces and see each other as true brothers and sisters in the faith. At the time, St. John's was part of the United Baptist Association, an organization made up of white, black, Hispanic, and Chinese churches whose leadership had placed racial reconciliation on their agenda. The UBA had two ongoing projects: Hope Chapel, a church for homeless people located close to Charlotte's Uptown Men's Shelter, and the UBA Bible School, a six-week Bible school over the summer for children in the low-income Belmont neighborhood. In the early 1990s, St. John's worked with St. Paul, Park Road, Greater Mt. Sinai, Sardis Road, Antioch, Chinese, Christian Mission, Milford Hills, Mt. Carmel, and Wedgewood Baptist churches to build Hope Chapel. Here is the Litany of Dedication for Hope Chapel from March 15, 1992:

> Leader: Lord, we busted our buns getting this house built.
> People: We got a good tan in the process.
> Leader: Lord, we hit our fingers and stubbed our toes.
> People: We said a few questionable words in the process.
> Leader: Lord, we have built this house for the needy.
> People: We hope the bums don't burn it down.
> Leader: Lord, smite the unrighteous!
> People: Translated: don't let the bums play with matches.
> Leader: YO!
> People: Amen![1]

Hope Chapel, which seats about sixty people, still serves a congregation every week. Its current director, Kevin Lynch, opens it early, with coffee brewing. Some weeks there is a visiting minister, and some weeks one of the parishioners offers the message.

The UBA Bible School did not survive as long as Hope Chapel, but it was an inspiring effort. The concept was to offer activities and Bible lessons, along with food and play and crafts, to children in a low-income neighborhood for six weeks of the summer. The first year, we held it in the Police Athletic League's building and spent the summer without air conditioning, struggling to keep the children out of the boxing ring. Each church was supposed to host one week—providing curriculum, workers, food, activities, and transportation. Over the years, one by one, the churches dropped out. St. Paul offered space for the Bible school, and, as other churches lessened their involvement, St. John's and St. Paul took over much of the burden. St. John's members covered most of the transportation—many of them have stories of picking up children and ferrying them back and forth to St. Paul's over the six weeks of summer. We took large groups of children to Carowinds, to Crowder's Mountain, to the Broad River, to public parks and public pools. We brought our own children along and have happy pictures of our blond and blue-eyed toddlers playing alongside black-haired, brown-eyed babies. It was a herculean effort, but it did not seem to break down barriers between our churches.

When Freedom School (a brilliant summer literacy program that serves children who are identified by teachers as those who need support with literacy during the summer) came to Charlotte, we joined forces with them and strove to support their work instead of trying to continually create a system of our own. Freedom School, a program sponsored by the Children's Defense Fund, not only focuses on literacy but also offers students a connection to literature with characters and heroes from the African-American and Hispanic communities. Its success rate is phenomenal, offering a different way of learning to students who generally do not get much support, and offering young adults the chance to step into spaces of real responsibility as classroom leaders and administrators.

At the same time, the death knell of the UBA was already beginning to sound. The one worship event we shared through the UBA every year was a special service for Martin Luther King Jr. Day. It was held at a different church each year, with another church bringing their choir and several ministers sharing the podium. Sometimes there would be a black preacher, sometimes a white preacher. After each service, there was a reception where, invariably, the church members from each church in attendance would stand around having lovely conversations and saying, "Why don't we do this more often?" And why not? We could all see how much we had in common—all of us Christians, all of us veteran churchgoers. I have more in common with an eighty-year-old black man who has gone to church all his life than I do with many of my white contemporaries who do not live a life of faith. Over the years, though, fewer churches participated in the Bible school; fewer came to the MLK service. When, finally, St. Paul stopped participating, the only black church left in the UBA was Greater Mt. Sinai, and only three of the white churches continued their involvement: Park Road, Sardis, and St. John's.

While all of this was going on, I was beginning my ministry as minister to children and families at St. John's. Part of that position, I thought, would include working with black churches. I began my work at Gardner-Webb University's School of Divinity and found a diverse population there, which seemed like a good sign. I began to work with a woman who led the children's choir at a nearby church that was predominantly black. I showed up with my children and my guitar to be part of some programs she was doing. And then I started to feel what I had felt before at NAACP meetings: I was not really welcome. There was nothing overt. Nothing was said outright to me. No one was rude or unkind, but I was clearly in this woman's space, and my guitar and I were not what she was looking for.

The Grace of Others

Of all the efforts I have witnessed toward racial reconciliation in my time as an adult, I can only name two that were successful. One is Hope Chapel, which is still doing amazing work each week. The other is neither a program nor something instigated by a church; it is the quiet work of a lovely couple, John and Elma Thomas. After retiring as educators and ministers, John and Elma, a black couple living in Charlotte, decided to visit and then to join St. John's Baptist Church. It says very little about St. John's that they joined this church: we passed the minimum requirement of human beings to be decent and kind toward newcomers. I think most of us were frankly stunned that such a lovely black couple would want to join our church. Tom Peacock, a white friend of mine who had been a member of St. John's since the 1940s and was the very definition of "pillar of the church" (and who died in spring 2018), often talked about the period after St. John's opened its membership to black people. He said, "We weren't as cute as we thought we were." In other words, no black people joined. St. John's didn't change anything to make black people feel welcomed; we simply said, "We will tolerate you as long as you do everything our way." There was no change in music or format, no change in staff, no acknowledgment of wrongdoing in the past.

John was a talker, and he loved the preaching of our senior pastor at the time. Elma is a retired schoolteacher who is fiercely intelligent and very quiet. She reminds me of Mrs. Amos, who kept me in line at in my first job as a teacher. Elma tells me that she heard Dr. Jonnie McLeod (an extraordinary leader at St. John's and in the Charlotte community) speak one time. When she and John began looking for a church after they retired, they decided to try St. John's. Upon their arrival, they were welcomed by a tall, friendly woman (who, as it turns out, is Betsy Almond), who walked them to Jonnie McLeod's Sunday school class and talked congenially with them as they navigated through the church. Elma says, in a rather kind and under-stated way, "White people aren't always warm," expressing something different she found at St. John's. Elma got involved with our work with our South Sudanese friends, helping them with their English at several teaching sessions. She came to our first women's retreat, and she and John both joined a Sunday school class, becoming part of a circle of friends.

John and Elma were members for several years before John became ill and passed away. One of the greatest gifts John and Elma and their family gave to St. John's was holding his funeral in our sanc-tuary. I had the great privilege of being asked to lead the service for that day and offer the eulogy. At the time, I had never been part of an African-American funeral service. I am pretty sure that St. John's had never hosted a funeral for a black member before. It was an amazing service, with the order of worship frequently interrupted by the need for someone else in the congregation to stand up and speak to how wonderful John was and what he had meant in that person's life. John died on the day President Barack Obama was awarded the Nobel

Prize. After I mentioned that John would have been proud to know that President Obama had been honored in that way, the funeral director thanked me and made mention of my comment several more times during the course of the service. I spent the service amazed at the grace the family showed in putting up with my ignorance of how they needed the service to be; they knew how little we knew, and they still invited us into that intimate family moment.

What St. John's got right, and what many other churches get right, is working on the micro scale. We knew how to be friendly and welcoming; we knew the work of being family inside a church community. We knew how to invite Elma and John Thomas in, to welcome their perspective, to show up with visits at their home, and to be present with prayer at hospital beds. We knew how to do all the things that involve treating individual human beings with equality and kindness, and we did them. What we did not do, what we and most other churches have struggled in doing, is work on the macro scale. We had no conversations that dealt with our systems; issues in the Charlotte community; and problems like injustice, inequality in the schools, substandard housing, and gentrification of black neighborhoods. We are just starting to have those conversations. Many of the churches I know believe they are past issues of race because they have members who are racial minorities. This assumption contributes to the persistent nature of our issues as it deals only with individuals, conveniently sidestepping systems and the need to walk through difficult conversations in order to truly be on the other side of them.

Things Fall Apart

The Thomases get credit for stepping in at St. John's. Since they joined, a few other black members have joined as well. And while, as I said, St. John's gets credit for being a warm and welcoming community, it is really the grace and trust of those who joined that should be credited for their membership here. Truly, until the last year, race was not a topic on the table at St. John's. Over the years, I have been in many conversations about our efforts to work together with black churches, and they all end the same way: Why didn't it work? Why didn't they want to talk things through with us?

Why did they disappear? Usually, it came down to the same middle-school-level question that I have asked myself many times: Why don't they like us?

During the last seven years, I have taken many training courses on race offered by various organizations. I will not try to recreate them here, as they are experiences and not textbooks.[2] What I can tell you is actually best summed up in a recent work by James Cone, theologian at Union Seminary in New York. In *Martin & Malcolm & America: A Dream or a Nightmare*, Cone's book about Martin Luther King Jr. and Malcolm X, he talks about the commonalities of the two men's theologies. Cone says,

> As different as Martin's and Malcolm's religious communities were, Martin's faith, nonetheless, was much closer to Malcolm's than it was to that of white Christians, and Malcolm's faith was much closer to Martin's than it was to that of Muslims in the Middle East, Africa, or Asia: this was true because both of their faith commitments were derived from the *same* [italics Cone's] black experience of suffering and struggle in the United States.[3]

Cone talks about King embodying his faith and says that, for King, it was lived out in

> what he did and said about justice and love between blacks and whites and about God's will to realize the American dream, reconciling, as brothers and sisters, the children of former slaves and former slaveholders. King was not an academic theologian; he was a theologian of action, a theologian of liberation (in the best sense) whose thinking about God was developed in his efforts to achieve freedom and dignity for black people.[4]

To me, King's theology is strikingly different from the evidence of white theology presented in Dr. Broach's sermon, which I mentioned in the previous chapter. Dr. Broach felt called to admonish his people against a "silly optimism" and a theoretical faith. He was begging them to wake up. Cone speaks of the pragmatic, active faith of King and of Malcolm X, who saw the work of God as part of daily life, part of justice, and part of who they were as people. All those trainings in which I took part are about the stark realities of systemic racism, which white people have the luxury of ignoring and black people must live with every day.

St. John's work toward racial reconciliation has met with failure after failure. We have made little progress despite our belief in our own good intentions. I know and love the people of St. John's and accuse them of nothing I have not been guilty of myself. They have at least been trying, which is more than many white Christians can say. Many of you may have been trying—you may have the same litany of failed efforts, and you may have come to the point of frustration where you actually stopped trying because you couldn't understand why your efforts did not lead to more fruitful relationships or to healing in the culture of your city. Here are the questions to ask yourself in order to evaluate your work honestly:

1. Have you, as a white Christian, done the hard work of acknowledging your own privilege? Have you tamed your defensiveness and the voices in your head that want to justify all your actions?

2. Has your church or organization done the hard work of learning the truth of the history of race in your city? Have you acknowledged the ways in which you have been holding up the systems that work against black people in your city?

3. When you enter a room with other Christians who happen to be black, are you listening or talking? Are you aware of the way white voices often take over the conversation? Are you able to quiet yourself to listen?

Until the answer to those three questions is "Yes," then all the dinners, all the MLK worship services, and all the "dialogs" will be doomed to failure. And, like Saul as described in Dr. Broach's sermon, we will call in vain for Samuel to come rescue us.

Lessons

- *Our efforts fail for good reason: we are not truly listening to the struggles of black people because our privilege and power give us permission not to do so.*
- *It is the grace of the black people who willingly join our community, not merely the efforts of white tolerance, that moves us forward.*
- *Black theology in America has offered its proponents a theology of liberation and action—one which speaks to the circumstances in which they live and which leads them toward active pathways to change; white theology in America has offered its proponents a more theoretical approach to systems of belief, one which supports existing systems and does not promote change.*

Notes

1. From the files on Hope Chapel at St. John's. There is no record of who wrote the litany, but it clearly contains some inside jokes from the experience of building the chapel together.

2. "Souls of White Folks," Mecklenburg Ministries, 2010; "Coming to Ferguson," Fellowship of Reconciliation, 2015; "Do Not Be Afraid," Baptist Peace Fellowship of North America/Bautistas por la Paz, 2016.

3. James Cone, *Martin & Malcolm & America: A Dream or a Nightmare* (New York: Maryknoll, 1991) 122.

4. Ibid., 123.

Station Break for
Good Theology

5

Biblical Hospitality: A Botched Mission

When an alien resides with you in your land, you shall not oppress the alien. The alien who resides with you shall be to you as the citizen among you; you shall love the alien as yourself, for you were aliens in the land of Egypt: I am the LORD your God. (Leviticus 19:33-34)

The Theology of Hospitality

Jesus told a parable about a guy who is awakened in the middle of the night by his neighbor. At that time, there were few places where visitors could find food or shelter; people who traveled from home were dependent on individuals to welcome them, offering a place to stay and food to eat. The laws of hospitality demanded the care of guests for good reason: we offer such care to others because we have been recipients of hospitality in the past and because we might need it again one day. We're part of something larger than ourselves, and it is in our best interest to deal with others kindly. In Jesus' story, a knock on the door in the middle of the night wakes up a man and makes him crawl over his sleeping family to get to the door. The knocking neighbor says, "I have family visiting and I don't have any bread!" He's breaking the rules already—he has awakened his neighbor and the neighbor's whole family because *he* wasn't prepared for guests. But the rules of hospitality are so great and so powerful that he risks causing his neighbor to hate him in favor of getting some bread for his guests. Jesus' comment is that despite the fact that this knocking neighbor is an obnoxious jerk, the man will get out of bed to give him bread. It is a parable about persistence and about the powerful call to hospitality.

We tend to think about hospitality in terms of restaurants and hotels—the "hospitality industry." Some of us have taken courses from businesses that specialize in hospitality, and we've learned how to have informative signs and how to welcome those who enter. Those are certainly elements of hospitality, but they show little of the serious nature of biblical hospitality. It turns out that the theme of hospitality is *everywhere* in the Bible—not only the assumption of hospitality as part of the culture of the time but also as a central theology given to the people of God.

Many excellent books are available on this subject,[1] and my book is not an attempt to cover the topic exhaustively. It is important, though, to view the work of hospitality theologically. After all, the inhospitable behaviors that got us into racial strife have been expressed theologically, and that theology has been spread through the churches and pulpits of America.[2] Let's review what is evident in the written word of God about how we are to treat those who come from somewhere either racially or culturally different from us.

Status and Treatment of the Stranger

In the Bible, the person who is not born into the insider's clan or village is called the "stranger" or the "alien" or the "foreigner." The Hebrew word that is typically used is *ger*, which basically means "person who wasn't born here" or "not our tribe." Greek offers several words for the same idea: *xenos* (usually defined as "foreigner" or "stranger"); *parsikos* (a foreigner who lives in a place without the right of citizenship); and *parapidemos* (someone from a foreign country who lives side by side with natives).[3] The terms arose from a tribal society in which villages were small and people lived within a short radius of land together; everyone knew where everyone came from. What the Bible sets up immediately and in no uncertain terms is that foreigners have a legal and moral place among the people of God.

Although this is by no means the only example, Leviticus 19 offers a good way to explore some of the nuances of biblical hospitality.

Leviticus 19:33-34 says, first of all, that the alien has status in your land—he or she "shall be to you as the citizen among you"; in other words, this person who has not been born into your tribe still lives with your tribe and has the full rights of a citizen in your land. There are legal rights and privileges that come with citizenship, and they are offered to "the alien who resides with you." Furthermore, there are some things that are not permitted for you in regard to the alien:

1. You are not allowed to hate them. You have to love them as you love yourself.
2. You are not allowed to oppress them.

There is also a reason given for why you will treat them as full citizens, why you will not oppress them, and why you have to love them: "for[4] you were aliens in the land of Egypt." And, in case you missed the power behind the statement, it is signed, "I am the LORD your God."

Think about the first theology offered by the Bible—where does everything come from? God. God is the founder, creator, builder, architect, owner, manager, operator, head honcho, and land-lord of every single thing there is. That is the identity of God.

Let's try another verse: Psalm 24:1.

The earth is the LORD's and all that is in it,
the world, and those who live in it.

The Bible, from the very beginning, covers the themes of ownership and property—everything we have (body, house, car, land, children, stocks, naming rights for a star) belongs to God. We are borrowing the use of it all, but there is not a single thing on this world, or any other, that belongs to us. And, like any landlord, God makes the rules. The rules are that everyone is a full citizen, that no one gets to hate anyone else for being different, and that, in fact, we are to make sure everyone else has what we have (which is what loving someone like yourself means).

Absolutely none of this theology has anything to do with a political party that is or was or ever will be. It is neither democratic nor socialist nor communist; no political organizational model fits with the theology of biblical hospitality. This is good theology that comes out of an understanding of a pervasive teaching from Scripture, and it holds up to scrutiny in lived experience.

Pervasiveness in Scripture

It would actually be easier to list the books of the Bible that make no mention of biblical hospitality and the call to welcome the stranger than to make a list of books that contain at least one reference to those ideas. Personally, I found about 140 places in the Bible that call on followers of God to care for the strangers in their midst.

There are those in Genesis and Exodus, which establish the connection between the people of Israel and the land, and which tell the story of the people being saved from oppression—brought out of a land where they were the foreigners—by God.

There are those in the books of law, which clearly point out that it is against the rules for us to oppress outsiders—no matter what it is that makes someone an outsider.

There are verses about justice and God's right to be in charge of justice, and verses which delineate, specifically, how justice should look, like Jeremiah 22:3-5:

> Thus says the LORD: Do justice and righteousness, and deliver from the hand of the oppressor him who has been robbed. And do no wrong or violence to the resident alien, the fatherless, and the widow, nor shed innocent blood in this place. For if you will indeed obey this word, then there shall enter the gates of this house kings who sit on the throne of David, riding in chariots and on horses, they and their servants and their people. But if you will not obey these words, I swear by myself, declares the LORD, that this house shall become a desolation.

They come from the mouth of God and the lips of Jesus. If repetition counts for anything (and, in literature, it most certainly does), then this theme of avoiding oppression has to be acknowledged as one of the most important in the whole of Scripture.

Biblical hospitality involves preparation (as in God preparing a city, Jesus preparing a place, the disciples preparing a room for Passover); it involves protection (as in Lot protecting his visitors from harm, the people of God protecting strangers from oppression, or God protecting strangers from oppression); it involves welcome and inclusion (as in making strangers into full citizens, making strangers into coworkers or part of the one body of Christ); it involves identifying with strangers (as in the call to empathize because we have been strangers too, in the recognition that none of this is ours anyway, and in seeing the face of Jesus in every single person we meet).

A while back, I picked up a book of writings by Dr. Thomas Buford Maston, a Christian theologian who wrote primarily in the middle of the twentieth century. I had read Maston before and appreciated his commitment to biblical themes as a basis for understanding a Christian moral ethic for living. In a writing about Christians and the issue of race, presented in Atlanta for the Home Mission Board of the Southern Baptist Convention in 1946, Maston said,

> The future of the Christian cause not only in the South but in the world will be determined, to a considerable degree, by what the Christians of the South do in the immediate future about the race situation. Are we going to attempt honestly to apply Christian principles to the race problem? If not, how can we expect others to continue to respect our Christian claims or to hear and accept the message we proclaim?[5]

Maston continued, "It is the church's business to be in the vanguard of the moral forces of society," and the great tragedy would be "for the churches of Christ to surrender their moral leadership to some social agency, political party, or labor organization."[6] In later writings, Maston invoked the story of Peter and Cornelius and applied the story of Ham to the issues of race in his own time, concluding that God is unprejudiced about human beings, and therefore "We should be impartial; we should not play favorites."[7] He found "no valid biblical or theological defense for the segregation pattern."[8] Finally, after exhaustively showing that, biblically speaking, there can be no justification for seeing one race as superior to another, Maston pointed out that the idea of superiority or inferiority is in fact irrelevant. He reminded readers that "The Christian religion says the strong should serve the weak. It is a fundamental Christian principle that privilege and power are never to be used selfishly," making any argument for different treatment of any member of any race indefensible in terms of the Christian faith.[9]

If we are honest with ourselves, our lived experience will show us that our lack of hospitality (understanding that hospitality is no small thing) has caused all of us enormous damage. In Angie Thomas's book *The Hate U Give*, one of the characters explains the meaning of "thug life": "Pac said Thug Life stood for The Hate U Give Little Infants Fucks Everybody. T-H-U-G-L-I-F-E. Meaning what society gives us as youth, it bites them in the ass when we wild out. Get it?"[10]

More than a hundred years ago, Frederick Douglass warned us that slavery was a cancer for all of us, a disease that destroyed our whole society. We've seen how our injustices have exploded in our faces, and how our silence leads to the death of young people. Our faith is not one which permits us to continue in self-imposed blindness—it is one of the few things we are not permitted. If we would call ourselves "Christ-ians," we have to open our eyes to the injustice we enact—there is no faith that is not lived in the world.

Throughout Christian history, we can observe the same pattern: Christians build a community of insiders; someone brings an outsider to the table; everyone says, "No, not them!" Good theology (in the form of some person who has read the Scripture) insists, "Yes, them too!" After much bashing of heads, inclusion ensues. There has never been a people group, made up of those identifying themselves by nationality or sexual identity or race or number of freckles, that some group of Christians has *not* come to recognize as completely and utterly welcome to the table, with full citizenship and no restrictions. Once included at the table, all the laws of hospitality apply—particularly protection. There has never been, nor is there now, any excuse for white Christian people to claim that they include black Christian people as "brothers and sisters in Christ" and then permit them to be vilified, ostracized, oppressed, excluded, or physically harmed in any way by any group.

Notes

1. See, for example, Arthur Sutherland, *I Was a Stranger: A Christian Theology of Hospitality* (Nashville: Abingdon Press, 2006); and Amy Oden, ed., *And You Welcomed Me: A Sourcebook on Hospitality in Early Christianity* (Nashville: Abingdon Press, 2001).

2. I feel your resistance. I hate it, too. It makes me feel sick to my stomach to think that I have been part of allowing real, true, dangerous injustice to happen all around me. That I may have accepted privileges as a result of someone else being denied their basic, human rights. I hate it. But remember the earlier lessons: I don't carry all of it. I carry my part—my real privilege, my actual blindness. I carry the privilege of my community, along with my community. And, it is very good news for me that I can start making it right. Rather than wallow in self-pity for the ways people are accusing me of being a racist, I can own what I have actually done. And stop doing it. And accept God's forgiveness. And go forward.

3. Francis Brown, S. R. Driver, Charles A Briggs, "Stranger," *The Brown-Driver-Briggs Hebrew and English Lexicon* (Peabody MA: Hendrickson Publishers, 2004) 158.

4. The word "for" indicates causality—"This is the reason you have to do these things . . . ."

5. William Tillman, Rodney Taylor, and Lauren Brewer, eds., "Of One," *Both-And: A Maston Reader* (T. B. Maston Foundation for Christian Ethics, 2011) 157.

6. Ibid., 157–58.

7. Ibid., 158.

8. Ibid.

9. Ibid., 167.

10. Angie Thomas, *The Hate U Give* (New York: Harper Collins, 2017).

The Challenge

"You've got to have something to eat and a little love in your life before you can hold still for any damn body's sermon on how to behave." (Billie Holiday)

Walking in Missouri, Part 1: In Which I Go to Ferguson in Spite of My Better Judgment

August 2015 was the one-year anniversary of the death of Michael Brown, a young man who, though he was unarmed, was shot six times by a Ferguson, Missouri, police officer, his body left lying in the street for four hours. His death sparked in Ferguson a movement that continues today. What follows is the narrative of my experiences in Ferguson in 2015. It is offered here as part of my understanding of what the work of racial reconciliation will entail if white Christians are to start doing it properly. The piece is printed here largely as I wrote it after I returned home in 2015, but it also includes some new reflections.

I did not want to go to Ferguson, Missouri. When I heard about the possibility of going at Peace Camp (an event sponsored by the Baptist Peace Fellowship of North America/Bautistas por la Paz), the two sides of my brain began a debate that continues through this moment as I write this reflection. I have paid attention to the events in Ferguson for many reasons. I was a public school teacher for eleven years in Charlotte-Mecklenburg schools, and many of my students were black. Some of them lived middle-class lives and some dealt with the realities of poverty, but from all of them I heard the facts of being black in America, such as getting pulled over for "driving while black." I've worked with Habitat for Humanity, with Charlotte Family Housing, and with groups like QC Family Tree for many years, and I know that white people and black people are not treated the same by our systems of education, justice, finance, or even faith.

In addition, in the last two years, I have had a young black man living in my house as one of my children. I cannot adopt him—his mother is both alive and a wonderful person. She is a South Sudanese refugee, though, and her realities include struggles with language and education that have made it impossible for her to get the kind of job that pays a living wage for her and her family. Our boy wants to go to college, so he has been living with us through high school. It's his family's and our family's goal that we help him with homework and with extracurricular activities so that higher education is a possibility for him. As I have gone about the task of raising a black boy in my home, I have noticed the different messages I have to give him about his behavior in public. He has a mischievous mind, and he likes to put on one of our ski masks and talk about going out in public. When he does this, I am absolutely terrified by the thought that he might do it—not because I think for one second that he is interested in breaking laws. He isn't. I am terrified because he is a large black male, and I am afraid that if he wears a ski mask in public, someone will shoot him. This is not a fear I deal with for any of my other children (who are white). I never had to say to my 6-foot-5-inch white son, "You can't wear that ski mask in public—someone might shoot you if you do."

And, so, I have been paying attention to the events in Ferguson, to the stories about what happened between Michael Brown and Darren Wilson, about how Michael Brown's body was treated and how the people in Ferguson have reacted, and part of me thought I should go and see for myself what the realities might be, as much as I could see them as an outsider. I am not immune to fear, and I feared Ferguson. I am not generally terrified of confrontation, but this situation, with its potential for violence, terrified me. So I tried not to go. I have this problem, though, with something I perceive to be the voice of God. Sometimes this voice tells me to do things, and I am almost never happy about the things this voice tells me to do.

When I left college, I had no plans to be a minister, I had never heard of South Sudan, and I was not particularly fond of children. I ended up being a minister to children who goes to South Sudan. Go figure. But this voice was telling me something about Ferguson, something powerful about what it meant for that young man to lie in the street for four and a half hours, something spiritual about what has been happening there since that event. My friends in the Baptist Peace Fellowship of North America were offering to sponsor a team to go to Ferguson, to be part of the anniversary of the death of Michael Brown, to be trained in civil disobedience, and to participate in a Moral Monday event. Despite all my efforts to avoid it, I ended up going to Missouri. In August. To get arrested.

The training materials we were given by the organizers in Ferguson included a strong message for white people: you need to keep your mouth shut. Here's the problem—white people are used to being in charge; we are used to being listened to. When we speak in a group of younger people or people from different races, we take over the conversation. When I read the admonition, I thought, "Yep. We do that." Our voices silence ideas from younger people and hinder strategies from people of different cultural origins. So I decided I would make it my spiritual discipline to shut up. This task was difficult—I felt that I had earned the right by my work and my presence to be part of the conversation. But what became clear from the first night of our delegation's time together was that I was not really a welcomed presence. There were six African-American people on the trip, all college graduates and all younger than thirty, and five white people, including our trainer, only two of whom were older (a lady from Raleigh, who is in her early sixties, and me).

As we began our training for the act of civil disobedience, which might end in our arrest, on Monday, the overwhelming emotions in our rooms were fear and distrust. It reminded me of middle school, and I went into middle school mode for a little while. It was clear that my fellow delegates did not welcome me or my fellow white lady. I went to bed each night plagued with depressing, negative thoughts: "They don't like me." "What am I doing here?" "I don't like them back." And then, one morning, I realized two things: (1) I am not in middle school. I didn't come to make friends. (2) I cannot contribute ideas, but because I am middle-aged, I probably make more money than the combined incomes of most of these young people, and I can cook breakfast. So I used my food allotment money and bought eggs and flour and milk and sausage and bacon and cheese and orange juice and coffee. And I made them breakfast. In my fifty-two years of life, I have learned the spiritual nature of food and the importance of the ministry of feeding people, so that's what I decided I could do. And I went to the training. And I shut up.

The training was unlike anything I'd ever experienced. One day, we went to a local church where we were met by several of the young people who had been part of the movement there in Ferguson. Many had been there the whole year, standing toe-to-toe with police in full riot gear. Some had been part of Black Lives Matter, a grass-roots movement that has arisen out of the growing realization that unarmed black Americans are being killed by armed policemen with impunity. Some had been in Baltimore and other cities; most had been part of protests; almost all had been tear-gassed.

For the training, several of them acted as "police," using their lived experience to embody what we could expect from the local law enforcement officials. We marched down the aisle, singing "We Shall Overcome," and then we sat on the stage floor with our arms linked. One young man came up to us and started yelling. I don't remember what he said, but he was terrifying. He started pulling our arms apart. My only tactic was to go limp; I had seen that in films about the civil rights movement and the Vietnam protests. Then they talked to us about what it was like to be tear-gassed and how to care for your skin and eyes if that were to happen. None of their instructions offered me any comfort. It all felt surreal, like a game we were playing or a fantasy we were living out. No part of my brain was ready to accept that this was the actual reality of the whole week.

In the evenings, there were meetings and some gatherings with speeches. We heard from Reverend Osagyefo Sekou quite a bit. He is a tiny individual, wound tightly like an industrial-strength metal spring. I came to admire both his courage and his intent. More than once, he talked about how he listened to the young people in this movement (a fact that was observable in the days to follow). He talked about how the Black Lives Matter movement puts the most vulnerable person in our society—specifically a black, transgender woman—at the forefront of the goals of the movement. The idea is that if a black, transgender woman is safe, then the rest of us should be safe as well. Rev. Sekou can be fiery in his sermons. I heard him speak at Peace Camp, and his anger poured out of him with every word; but in the training and in the down times, I observed him to be kind, gentle, and thoughtful. There is much to admire in his work.

We heard one night from Dr. Cornell West, who is a lovely, funny, and challenging speaker. He called us to courage and to moral outrage on behalf of our brothers and sisters there in Ferguson who would be at the center of why we were doing what we came to do. More than his speeches, though, Dr. West inspired me with his actions: he marched in the front. Whatever the police were going to lob at us (and the history of that place showed that peaceful protesters were met with rubber bullets, tear gas, batons, and police in full riot gear), he was first in line. For me, whose dearest hope was that I would be on the sidelines, cheering him on and not actually *in* the line with him, he offered strength and courage that I still deeply admire.

I also met a professor from a local seminary, a woman younger than I, who showed us a picture of the bruise that resulted when she was shot by a rubber bullet at a protest. The bruise covered her entire stomach. She is a minister and a teacher who was part of a peaceful protest, and she was shot in the stomach with a rubber bullet.

As the day of our civil disobedience approached, it was clear that I still had not earned much of a place among my fellow protesters. Not being young, I couldn't be cool. Not being black, I could not share in the suffering that manifested itself in the sounds of one young woman comforting another, quietly crying together in our darkened dorm room. We began to talk seriously about who was willing to do what; we actually signed a form about our willingness to be arrested. Barbara, the other white woman and an intrepid individual if there ever was one, was more than willing to be arrested. She already had been arrested in Raleigh, North Carolina, during the Raleigh Moral Monday action there, which protested the gerrymandering the

North Carolina state legislature has done to keep itself "red," and the unconscionable laws that same legislature has enacted to keep black people and poor people from voting. She was excited about the prospect. And, as we were encouraged to have a partner so that someone in the crowd was always looking out for us, she was mine. I said I, too, was willing to be arrested although my hope was that it would not be necessary. We went to bed pretty quietly Sunday night, still not knowing exactly what the action would be. As I went to sleep in my little bunk bed, I was not pleased with God. "This was your idea," I said, turning over grumpily for a fitful night of sleep.

7

Walking in Missouri, Part 2: In Which I Get Arrested and Get to Keep My Shoelaces

Monday, the day for our Moral Monday action, our moment of civil disobedience to get the attention of the nation, finally arrived. I was not far from a state of panic, which I tried to control through quiet conversations with those around me. There was no part of me that wanted to go to the protest. We had not even been told what we would do, and I did not know how I would react if I were asked to do something that I did not believe was right. What message would I convey to these young people if suddenly I said, "I can't do this"? What if I chickened out? At the cathedral in downtown St. Louis, we practiced for the event. Again, we rehearsed linking arms and sitting down; again, we had practice police, and one of the trainers informed me that she had broken the arm of the person with whom I was linked in our practice protest. This news did not improve my state of mind. As we began to sing inspirational songs and line up for the march, terror seized me again.

I will take a moment here to talk about my buddy. As I mentioned, we had been encouraged to partner up for the march so that someone was watching out for us as we went into the fray. Barbara and I had talked about whether or not we were willing to be arrested. Over the course of the time we were there, I had come to believe it was important for me to volunteer to be arrested. First, it seemed that I had a lot less at stake than the young people around me did. While I knew people in my home church would be unhappy with me (and, in fact, some were quite unhappy with me, particularly because my name and picture got in a paper as one who was arrested), I also believed that I would not be fired. At fifty-two, I have pretty much established who I am with those who hire me or offer me space to complete programs in their schools. If they decided, after I was arrested, that the proverbial camel's straw had been acquired, then I would go on to other things. The other reason to get arrested was more pressing: clearly, before I came to Ferguson, I had not earned the right to be part of the discussion about how badly we handle race and issues surrounding race in America. I decided that if being arrested were the price, if being arrested while I was standing up for black lives and fair treatment and the intervention of the federal government into a corrupt system were necessary, then it was something I should do. That Monday morning, I realized that despite the fact that I said I would get arrested, despite the fact that I had agreed to do so, I was having cold feet. I did *not* want to confront armed police. I did *not* want to experience pepper spray or tear gas. I did *not* want angry police dealing with me harshly. I did *not* want to break a law (or even a rule) in order to get myself arrested.

My intrepid buddy Barbara, however, felt otherwise. We marched from the cathedral to the Department of Justice building, chanting, "Black Lives Matter!" and "This is what democracy looks like!" and listening to the beat of the drums at the front of the crowd. Barbara was disturbed that we were so far back, but I reassured myself that maybe, in the back like this, we could make our statement without having to be arrested. When we arrived at the DOJ building, Homeland Security had erected police barriers—the metal fences that are too tall to jump and have no bars to step on to help one get over them. I eyed them with relief, thinking my buddy and I to be a tad too old to jump over such barriers.

Being with a group of clergy, I stopped my dithering long enough to enjoy the way that my fellow clergy confront power: with a scroll. I just love clergy. They marched toward the government building, and what they wanted to do was to give them a scroll, the contents of which asked for the federal government to intervene in Ferguson, to investigate the abuses people were registering against police, and, as a matter of civil rights, to address the discrepancies between the way white people in the St. Louis area are treated and the way black people are treated. They wanted to anoint each other and the building with oil, to call down the divine presence to be with those in power and help them see their black citizens as equal and deserving of the same rights as others. I have reflected since that moment that a smart government official would not have put up barriers; instead, he or she would have come down to meet the clergy. A smart government official would have met them at the top of the stairs and said, "Welcome to the Department of Justice! What's that you've got there . . . a scroll? Well, come on up to my office and let's take a look at it." A smart government official would have given Cornel West and Rev. Sekou and the other leaders a tour of the building and thirty minutes of his or her time, and then sent them on their way. That is not what they did.

Instead of diffusing the situation, they escalated the stakes at every turn. Against a group of clearly identifiable clergy (wearing robes and stoles and collars and, in some cases, actual vests that read "Clergy"), they had set up fencing and guards armed to the teeth. Our group was prepared to escalate things as well—it was our intention to get some of our group arrested (which, as I said, is why a smart official would have denied us that goal). After reading the scroll and anointing the building, several of the leaders of our group went over the barriers. I stood back, thinking Barbara was standing beside me, until the moment when I saw her in front of me—going over the barrier.

My reaction was not one of joy. But she was my buddy, and I was damned if I was going to let her and the rest of the group down. So, gracelessly and with much help from the younger members of my delegation, over the metal fence I went. At first there was more clapping and chanting and singing while Homeland Security officers glared at us with their hands on their Tasers. Then we moved around them and sat in front of the doors. We linked arms. We chanted.

Someone came up behind me and got my full name and birthday so they would know who was in jail. And then the St. Louis police showed up. I heard someone being arrested behind me. Then a man said in my ear, "You are being arrested. Put your hands behind your back." Although I had practiced noncooperation, I made the split-second decision to cooperate as I had used up all the courage I had for one event.

I put my hands behind my back and the officer slipped the plastic handcuffs on my wrists. He tightened the one on my right wrist, then tightened it again until it was painful. He put the cuff on my left wrist and, as he pulled it tight, it slipped onto my hand, so that when he tightened—twice—it went around the meat of my hand, missing my wrist completely. This hurt badly, and as they stood me up I realized that I could not feel my fingers.

"These cuffs are too tight," I said. "They are hurting me. I am not resisting. Please cut these off and do this again—these are cutting off my circulation."

At this point, the fear and humiliation of the day and of that moment, matched by the pain in my hands, overwhelmed me and I dissolved into tears. I had not meant to cry. My buddy was defiant; she stood up and yelled, "Black lives matter!" when they arrested her. I did not. I was so upset that they ushered me quickly inside, somehow unable to locate a cutter to remove the cuffs. Twice, one of the officers called me "dear." In my brain, I said, "Call me 'dear' one more time." But I was crying. And I did not say it out loud.

By the time they finally cut the cuffs off my hand (leaving a mark that lasted for a couple of days), my anger had returned. Before they took my phone away, I snapped a picture of my hand in case it was truly injured (it wasn't—just bruised). I had control of myself again, but I think they didn't want to deal with me anymore. I was not searched (unlike most of the other people, especially the young black women who were arrested with me). I even got to keep my shoelaces, which earned me some disdain among my cell-mates. "White lady tears," they said. The rest of my time in the jail was uneventful. The DOJ people who were processing us were uninterested in the whole thing. They were far more concerned with getting to their pizza than they were with us. They treated us with derision and impatience and got us all out in a matter of six or seven hours. I have a thing—call it a trigger—about bullies. These guys seemed accustomed to using bullying behavior to get their jobs done. It did not endear them to me.

They gave us our tickets (mine was a $125 fine for blocking a doorway) and ushered us out, the way you would people who came to a party to which they had not been invited. When we left the building, we sat or stood for about an hour in the same spot where we had been arrested seven hours earlier. Somehow, it was not illegal to sit there anymore. By the time our group got to dinner that night, we were all kind of giddy with the adrenaline of the event. It was the first meal we shared in which we were truly one group. We went to Steak & Shake to celebrate the birthday of one of the young women (who also happened to be one of the African-American people in our group to get arrested). We bought her a large milkshake.

I am still a long way from completely processing all that happened during our time in St. Louis and what it might mean. I find that I do not regret having been arrested—I am seriously considering getting tattoos around my wrists with the words "Place handcuffs here" written under them for future arrests. Many people have said they are proud of me, many have expressed confusion about why I went, and a few are angry and want to talk about how Michael Brown deserved to be shot because he fought the police, or how protest is not the way to effect change. As always, I appreciate working for a church that offered me the opportunity to follow what felt like every other call I have ever felt from God—right down to the part where I didn't want to do it.

Questions remain for me. What will I do with this knowledge I have gained? How can I translate this experience into something that benefits my children, my church, my community, my country? I am not sure how to answer those questions yet. I gained some powerful friendships, though. I have no idea how or to what degree our lives will intersect again, but there was something remarkably human and wonderful about the last twenty-four hours our group spent together. I was deeply compelled by the way the members of the Black Lives

Matter movement look after each other and work to stand up for each other. Their commitment to the most fragile people in their community is powerful and moving. It is my fervent hope that whatever else I did, whatever else *we* did as a group and a delegation, we proclaimed our belief that Black Lives Matter and that we are willing to go some distance to make sure the world hears it from our lips.

8

September in Charlotte: In Which It All Comes Home

The following is a reflection on the events of September 20–21, 2016, in Charlotte, North Carolina, after Keith Lamont Scott was shot by police there. On the night he was shot, protests erupted around the city; on the second night, a more formal protest happened in uptown Charlotte. This account is meant to be my reflections of the events and not to represent an authoritative recounting of what happened. Others saw it differently, and their accounts would be their own. This one is mine.

Charlotte, despite its lack of violent protests or riots over the past several years, has not been a progressive force in the movement toward racial equality. In a program on May 17, 2016, at St. John's Baptist Church, with members from St. John's, Friendship Missionary Baptist Church, Providence Baptist Church,[1] and the public in attendance, Tom Hanchett, a local historian, outlined the egregious harms perpetrated on African Americans in Charlotte over the last 116 years. For the purposes of understanding the specific harms in Charlotte visited by the white community and the wealthy community on African Americans (simultaneous with harms visited on poor people of all pigments), the main issues Hanchett outlined were these:

• In 1875 Charlotte was *not* segregated by race or by economic status.

- In the period after the Civil War, poor whites and poor blacks joined in a "fusion" of power in the Republican party to vote out the wealthy who had held power.
- In the 1890s, an economic downturn and the loss of their powerful seats of leadership made the wealthy look for tactics to divide the "fusion."
- White leadership quickly went to work to demonize African Americans and to remove voting rights (using methods like poll taxes, literacy tests, and propaganda).
- Red-lining became a federal program of approval for banks to invest in certain neighborhoods and to refuse loans in "bad" neighborhoods, specifically those with African Americans and immigrants.
- The GI Bill gave low-interest mortgages to white veterans, but African-American veterans were refused access.
- The African-American neighborhood of Brooklyn was overtaken by whites, requiring 1,000 people to be displaced from their homes, businesses to close (most of which never reopened), and more than a dozen churches to be moved out of the neighborhood.
- Communities such as Myers Park were created as gated communities with the clear purpose of providing space for wealthy whites to live while keeping out African Americans and poor whites.

A specific incident that Hanchett described is particularly memorable: on a float in a parade just before the election of 1900, an African American stood at a ballot box. Beside him, white men held a gun to his head. The intentional demonizing of African-American males is illustrated in the cartoon from the *Raleigh News and Observer* of that year. Hanchett also showed an image of a map of Charlotte from 2016, displaying where people live based on race and economics: the wedge of wealthy whites is to the south and north of the city; the crescent of poorer whites and African Americans goes around the center of the city with clear lines of demarcation between the two. Charlotte is a divided city and was made so intentionally over the last 100 years.[3]

In addition to its entrenched segregation in neighborhoods, Charlotte has become increasingly segregated in its schools. In the 1990s, the city reinstituted the desegregation of its schools in a reopening of *Swann v. Charlotte-Mecklenburg Schools*, the 1972 landmark decision that had mandated the desegregation of schools in Charlotte. Prior to *Swann*, CMS had some exemplary schools (East Mecklenburg High School and West Charlotte High School, to name two) that had made tremendous strides in mastering diversity and at which busing had helped to create thriving academic communities for students from all areas of Charlotte. The reopening of the case, brought by six white families, led to an examination of the still deeply entrenched distinctions between what African-American students were offered through CMS and what white students received.[4] After the resegregation of Charlotte Public Schools, which began in the 90s and has since become the ongoing reality of public schools in that city, poverty in Charlotte became more deeply entrenched in certain neighborhoods. Title I schools began to serve populations that were 98 percent free and reduced lunch, and middle-class white students once again went to schools where they rarely, if ever, encountered black students in their classes. In a study conducted by researchers at Harvard University, Mecklenburg County was found to be, "In terms of income inequality, among the 5 percent of worst counties," and found that children who grow up poor in Mecklenburg County have a high likelihood of remaining so.[5]

Finally, as if these realities of history and economics were not enough, Keith Lamont Scott was shot and killed by a Charlotte police officer on September 20, 2016. That night, protesters took to the streets of Charlotte, creating the first angry mobs Charlotte has seen in the thirty years of my residence here. On the day after the shooting, the Charlotte Clergy Coalition for Justice, of which I am a member, was contacted by groups planning to lead a protest march that night and asked to invite clergy to be present for the protest, to provide a calm presence in the crowd. Along with about thirty other clergy, I responded to the call and went to the Little Rock AME Zion Church on McDowell and 7th Street to get instructions. We were asked to put a yellow ribbon around our arms to indicate that we were clergy and to walk with the crowd. The following are my observations of what happened, having walked with the crowd the entire way up to the use of tear gas by the police:

- The crowd gathered at Marshall Park, made up largely of black Charlotteans but also of some whites, including clergy.
- The crowd at Marshall Park was determined and angry but not violent.
- The crowd marched to Little Rock AME Zion, accompanied by police on bikes.
- At Little Rock, many in the crowd began to question why they would gather at a church and decided to move to the police station.
- The crowd moved to the police station, increasingly angry but still nonviolent.
- At the police station, the crowd began to talk of moving to the EpiCenter, a collection of shops, restaurants, and movie theaters in uptown Charlotte, just up Trade Street. At this point, most of the clergy had dispersed. Many were still in Marshall Park, talking to people and offering comfort; some had stayed around Little Rock, and others were around the police station.
- At the EpiCenter, most people began walking around talking to each other. Some moved into the EpiCenter, and some vandalism began happening, but still there was no violence.
- Within minutes, the police came down Trade Street in full riot gear, and the crowd moved to respond. The police were armed with tear gas, pellet guns, and batons.
- The clergy were asked to stand between the police and the protesters, which we did; as the police moved back up the street toward the Omni Hotel, the clergy stayed between them and the people, and the crowd followed the moving line of clergy and police.
- When the police turned into the Omni parking deck, some of the people followed and the police fired tear gas into the crowd. At that point, the crowd, though loud and angry, had shown no signs of violence; police continued to fire tear gas and rubber bullets into the crowd.

• Protesters continued to stay in the streets and to confront police, but I witnessed no violent acts toward police; there were acts of vandalism elsewhere downtown.

I found the events of that week exceptionally traumatizing. For one thing, I went uptown at the request of the Charlotte Clergy Coalition, an organization I belong to openly but that I was not sure anyone in my church (other than my direct supervisor) knew anything about. Also, especially after some of the conversations and events I experienced after I returned from Ferguson, I could not tell whether the majority of my church would be proud that I participated or ready to fire me for being there. The real issue, though, was the violence and fear created when the police showed up in riot gear. While I am not prepared to say that no violence would have happened if they had not come, I can say, because I was there at the EpiCenter before they arrived, that there was no violence happening around me until they came. I saw people in the EpiCenter, and they may have been vandalizing those buildings, but, and this is something I learned in Ferguson, people are more important than property. It never occurred to me until that time that what is happening in our culture is the valuing of property over people.

When the police came down the road, what I wanted to do— what I should have done—was run forward and kneel down in front of them in prayer. There were children in that crowd—not just teenagers (who are also children) but elementary-school-aged children whose parents had brought them to be part of a peaceful protest. Again, I felt hamstrung by not being a leader and by my own fears. When one of the other clergy, with whom I had been talking a moment before, said, "We are going to form a line between the police and the people," I joined him. We linked arms and formed a line, trying to put ourselves between the police and the people. I can tell you this much about riot gear: it does give permission for the person wearing it to detach from what is going on around him or her. The policeman in front of me—inches from my face—never looked at me or acknowledged our presence. He was listening to orders coming from somewhere else, and none of us factored into his next move. This had not been true of the police on bikes, who had followed us through the evening; they engaged with the crowd and talked with many of the marchers as they rode along.

The police line began to move. They reformed their ranks and marched back up toward the Omni Hotel. We accompanied them, keeping our line between them and the crowd as much as we could. For reasons known only to them, the police turned into the Omni garage, creating a traffic jam of people. Because I was at the doors, I can't speak to what happened inside the garage. But I do know that when the tear gas was fired, the crowd started to run. For those of you who haven't had this experience, tear gas stings your eyes; it is oily, and it gets on your clothes and in your hair. It takes a couple of showers to be rid of it completely. In this situation, I was again stunned by the lost opportunities to calm the situation. At any moment, the escalating events might have been quieted by one official coming forward and looking for the leaders in the crowd. Simply listening to them, holding back the police, and focusing on the safety of that crowd would have lessened the chances that someone would get hurt.

After the tear gas started, I gathered with a couple of the other clergy on a corner nearby. One of them was a young woman who has been in leadership in the movement, Rev. Robin Tanner. She had some of her parishioners with her, one with a young teenaged daughter. She needed someone to take them back to their car, and I leapt at the chance to do something productive that would get me out of that scene. After dropping off the mother and daughter, I went home and showered the whole experience off of my body. For me, the next day was almost as traumatizing as the night before. Person after person—some of them my friends—posted comments on Facebook. They said, "This is not my Charlotte." They said, "Those were not Charlotteans—they were thugs from out of town." Let me straighten out the record on this point: *I* was there. I walked with the protesters. I interviewed them and have the tapes to prove it. One young man whom I interviewed was the son of one of the policemen in the crowd; he told me how his father was proud of him for being there. These people brought their children with them to the protest.

They were Charlotteans. That *is* our Charlotte—it is the Charlotte we created.

I could not make myself go back uptown the next night. Many of those who were there Tuesday did go back, bravely, and stood with the protesters for several nights. The work of Charlotte Uprising, a group formed to support local actions for justice, continues in our city, and there is still much work to be done. Just this spring, when white parents got a glimpse of the proposed reassignment plan for Charlotte-Mecklenburg Schools, I witnessed a school board meeting where those indignant white parents had come to protest the very thought of their children being assigned somewhere besides their prominent white high school. Despite the protests, despite the absolute certainty that systems in Charlotte are unfair, the loudest voices in the white community still insist that they should be allowed to keep all of their privileges, no matter what. We have a long road ahead of us as we move toward racial reconciliation. And I understand better now how black people are exhausted with "dialogs" about it. The work that is left to do is the work of justice—it comes neither easily nor cheaply. But nothing will change until it is done.

Notes

1. St. John's and Providence are predominantly white churches; Friendship is predominantly black.

2. Tom Hanchett, "Melting Pot to Salad Bowl: Race in Charlotte Neighborhoods," lecture on May 17, 2016, at St. John's Baptist Church, Charlotte NC.

3. Ibid.

4. Katherine Chamblee, "Progressing Backward: The Re-Opening of *Swann v. Charlotte-Mecklenburg Schools*," Swarthmore College, www.swarthmore.edu/writing/progressing-backward-re-opening-swann-v-charlotte-mecklenburg-schools (accessed 23 January 2017).

5. Marshall Terry and Michael Tomsic, "New Research Shows Mecklenburg County among Worst for Economic Mobility," 6 May 2015, wfae.org/post/new-research-shows-mecklenburg-county-among-worst-economic-mobility (accessed 23 January 2017).

9

Southern Gentle Lady, Be Good

I preached this sermon on August 20, 2017, at St. John's Baptist Church. Before I preached this sermon, I had been on staff for almost sixteen years and a member for almost thirty. I had been part of the work St. John's had begun to do over the last year in racial reconciliation, and the sermon was received with much grace. Part of a sermon series on the Ten Commandments, it addresses the Ninth Commandment.

You shall not give false testimony against your neighbor. (Exodus 20:16)

Not many of you should become teachers, my fellow believers, because you know that we who teach will be judged more strictly. We all stumble in many ways. Anyone who is never at fault in what they say is perfect, able to keep their whole body in check. When we put bits into the mouths of horses to make them obey us, we can turn the whole animal. Or take ships as an example. Although they are so large and are driven by strong winds, they are steered by a very small rudder wherever the pilot wants to go. Likewise, the tongue is a small part of the body, but it makes great boasts. Consider what a great forest is set on fire by a small spark. The tongue also is a fire, a world of evil among the parts of the body. It corrupts the whole body, sets the whole course of one's life on fire, and is itself set on fire by hell. (James 3:1-6)

We all know the answer to this one question, no matter the circumstances under which it is asked: "Do these pants make me look fat?" The answer, of course, is, "No! You look great!" Right? There's no

world in which someone says, "Sorry, but you look like an adver-
tisement for a sausage factory in those things." And, when we come
to this next to the last commandment in our Decalogue, we tend to
think of it as being about honesty, don't we? Brutal honesty, where we
say things like, "Yes, you look fat in those pants." As it is stated, both
in Hebrew and in English, the actual commandment is "You shall
not bear false witness against your neighbor." The wording involves
legal language: "witness" or "testimony," words that would be used in
a court of law. And the last phrase, "against your neighbor," refers to
testifying falsely in such a way that it harms your neighbor.

Jesus made very clear who our neighbor is, didn't he? Who is our
neighbor? Not just everybody—this is not a general instruction to
"be nice to everybody" but a very specific task of actually reaching
out to those we would regard as strangers or aliens, those we would
ordinarily call our enemies. As usual, it is so much easier for us to
attend to minutia, such as the petty lies we tell to get by in a single
day, than it is for us to address the actual truth of what we have
done: that this commandment is almost always lost in translation.
Jesus, as always, is absolutely correct in the assessment of us that
involved splinters and logs—we would rather deal with splinters.
This penultimate commandment does not say, "Don't lie"; it is not
about politeness or social niceties at all. It's not about who took a
cookie or who broke the lamp. It is about justice—the thing we seek
when we go into a court of law. The thing God is about. The vital
component of righteousness that makes God a God of love. Justice.

Let's say, for example, that a person is witness to a crime. She has
seen a man attack another woman, beating her, taking her money,
and leaving her for dead. Let us further say that she is subpoenaed
by the court to tell what she saw. What if she doesn't go? Well, she is
then in trouble with the law. What if she goes but pretends that she
didn't really see anything or that she doesn't remember? What if the
man who did this crime, who was caught by the police, and whom
everyone knows is guilty cannot be convicted of the crime because
the woman will not testify to what she saw? That is what it means
to bear false witness. She caused harm to her neighbor, denying her

justice, by ignoring the truth, whatever her reason for doing so might have been.

I have been thinking about this sermon all summer because I knew what it had to be. I never know, until I hear it, what God will give me to say about a certain passage, but this one came early and I did not want to do it. About a month ago, I read about a book by James Cone, the wonderful theologian from Union Theological Seminary in New York. The book is called *The Cross and the Lynching Tree*. As you might imagine, it is a difficult book. I had already been thinking about a poem by Langston Hughes, which I have quoted in the title of the sermon. The poem is called "Silhouette" and it reads in part,

> Southern gentle lady,
> do not swoon,
> They've just hung a black man,
> In the dark of the moon.
> . . .
> Southern gentle lady,
> Be good!
> Be good![1]

I used to teach this poem when I taught American literature. I understood it to be about lynchings, which in my mind were rare occurrences that happened when mobs got out of hand, as in the incident in *To Kill a Mockingbird*. I never really tried to find out the truth about those lynchings—I assumed I knew. Cone's book would teach me otherwise.

In truth, lynchings were systematic, with more than 5,000 lynchings in a fifty-year period between 1880 and 1930 in the United States. They took place in just about every state in the nation, not just in the South. And they were known about at every level: senators, congressmen, ministers, bishops, supreme court justices—they all knew that these lynchings were happening, and they approved of them as a necessary method to keep down people who were thought to be dangerous just because of the color of their skin. Cone says, "To be black meant that whites could do anything to you or your people, and that neither you nor anyone else could do anything about it."[2]

Not only that, but these lynchings were not spur-of-the-moment events. They were announced in papers—hundreds and sometimes tens of thousands of people showed up at an event with a fair-like atmosphere. There was often a photographer who would take pictures of the cheering crowd, making the pictures into postcards and selling them for twenty-five cents apiece the next day so that people could send them to their relatives who could not attend. And as we sit here and take that in, I know you understand that no one in this room is being asked to atone for the sins of those people—no one in here was there. There is a very good chance that none of our parents participated in anything like this horrific event either. No. We are not addressing that today. Today, we are talking about bearing false witness. And in that respect, the white Christian church has an enormous problem.[3]

Although our particular church never housed ministers who called for hatred from the pulpit, although we have not been guilty of violent language or hate speech, we have also not believed our African-American brothers and sisters when they told us what was happening to them. We have not taught the truth of our history in our schools, nor have we insisted that it be taught to our children. We have not protested the egregious discrepancies between schools that are primarily white in Charlotte and schools that are primarily African-American. We have not borne witness to truth in search of justice.

Cone quotes several other theologians in his book. He quotes Rabbi Joachim Prinz, a German refugee to the US, who said, "When I was a rabbi of the Jewish community in Berlin under the Hitler regime . . . the most important thing I learned under those tragic circumstances was that bigotry and hatred are not the most urgent problems. The most urgent and most disgraceful, the most shameful, the most tragic problem is silence." Cone also quotes Reinhold Niebuhr, his predecessor at Union, who said, "I do mean to say this: that the bulk of the white . . . Christian majority in this country has exhibited a really staggering level of irresponsibility and immoral washing of hands, you know . . . I don't suppose that . . . all white people in Birmingham are monstrous people. But they're mainly silent people, you know. And that is a crime in itself." And he quotes James Baldwin, who said that most Americans "have been for so long, so safe and so sleepy, that they don't any longer have any real sense of what they live by. I think they really think it might be Coca-Cola."[4]

The point of Cone's book is that Christianity is a faith of the cross—the symbol of a first-century lynching. And while African Americans have for centuries now understood, deeply, the meaning of the sacrifice of the cross, because they were living it through oppression and through these horrible, systemic lynchings, white Christians have ignored this truth of the faith, actively participating in the false witness that our systems are not harming our brothers and sisters in ongoing and unconscionable ways. Cone quotes the black historian Lerone Bennett Jr., who said that African-American people understood "at the deepest level . . . what it was like to be crucified . . . . And more: that there were some things in this world that are worth being crucified for."[5]

In the book, Cone tells the story of Mamie Till Mobley, the mother of Emmett Till, who, as a fourteen-year-old boy visiting family in the South, was tortured and murdered and thrown in the river with a heavy piece of machinery tied to his body. Mamie insisted that her son's body be on display, with an open casket, for three days, exposing "his battered and bloated corpse" so that "everybody can see what they did to my boy." She spoke of a voice that came to her and said, "Mamie, it was ordained from the beginning of time that Emmett Louis Till would die a violent death. You should be grateful to be the mother of a boy who died blameless like Christ. Bo Till will never be forgotten. There is a job for you to do now." She told the press about her prayer: "Lord, you gave your son to remedy a condition, but who knows but what the death of my only son might bring an end to lynching."[6] And, in fact, the images of Emmett Till's face brought national and international attention to the problem, the pressure of which and the truth of which served to facilitate an end to that horrible period.

This is the power of truth. It is in this way that truth makes us free. It is not painless, and it is not comfortable. It requires that we sacrifice our apathy and our misguided attachment to our own "rightness." Mamie Till Mobley bore witness to truth.

Friday evening, as I drove home from delivering my son back to college, I listened to the Radiolab podcast. It is not the first time that I have been given the gift of a story before I was called on to preach. The story was about a newspaper in Tampa, Florida, that spent two to three years finding all the data on arrests and shootings in the state. In many ways, their findings were grim—throughout the state of Florida, which is 17 percent African-American, 40 percent of those who are arrested or who have violent encounters with law enforcement are African-American. Part of the story, though, was the good news about one police chief who has chosen to bear witness to truth.

Mike Chitwood, who is now the sheriff for the entire county, was then the chief of police in Daytona Beach. Daytona Beach is a city of 62,000 people and is often home to events such as Bike Week, with more than 500,000 motorcyclists, and the Daytona 500. In a six-year period between 2009 and 2014, the police in Daytona Beach had only two police shootings. Furthermore, annually, their breakdown of arrests and tickets matches their population; in other words, the police in Daytona Beach arrest and ticket people the same regardless of their race or skin color. When the interviewer asked Chief Chitwood how they managed that in such a short time period he said,

> When all these incidents were occurring in Ferguson and around the country, we did a mandatory training on race in policing for the entire PD. And basically, what we wanted all the officers to do was, number one, learn the history of the country. Because the history of the country is that we are a racist nation, no matter how you want to look at it. It started with moving the Indians off of their land with Manifest Destiny. When you look at Jim Crow laws, when you look at the Civil War and slavery, when you look at Bull Conner, for example, turning dogs and fire hoses loose on civil rights marchers. So it's important for officers to understand that. When you go into an African-American community,

you may think you talk and act in a way that is respectful and understanding, but in reality, you're not. But let's not think for a moment that there isn't bias in policing. Because there's bias, we all have bias in us. . . . How do we stop that bias from coming when we make a decision?[7]

Chitwood's tactic was acknowledgment, then training. He doesn't hire nineteen-year-olds; he hires veterans who have a cooler head and experience with extreme circumstances. He trains his people to keep distance between them and those who seem dangerous, giving the officers time to position themselves and to assess the situation. He has his officers get involved with the community—learn people's names and know who they are. In the last year, since he became the sheriff for his county, Chitwood has also been part of forming something called PERF, the Police Executive Research Forum, which published thirty Guiding Principles for the Use of Force. The first of their guiding principles is the sanctity of human life. Since that time, the ICP and the Fraternal Order of Police have both adopted some of those guidelines for use throughout the country.[8]

The point is that the truth does not deal in false dichotomies: it is possible to acknowledge wrongdoing without abandoning other truths. It is possible to defend one group of people without condemning another. To be people of truth, to be the people of the God of truth, is neither simple nor always pleasant. And, to our credit, we come back, week after week, to submit ourselves to uncomfortable and challenging words.

This past week, I had the chance to meet with my Circle of Hope[9] group. We have a wonderful group, and we met at the lovely home of Ken and Wanda Hungate, where we were all met with gracious hospitality. And I have to admit that I stole the conversation—I had to hear what my friends from Friendship would say about this topic. Fortunately, they offered me no out. There was no world in which they excused me from the task of broaching the topic of the way white Christians have borne false witness, both to our own complicity and to the realities of what is happening to our brothers and sisters. Our friend Timothy, one of the group members from Friendship Missionary Baptist, said this: "What if you tell them that they can be part of another person's salvation? What if you tell them that by acknowledging this truth, by speaking up, white people can be a part of saving us?" He invoked Dietrich Bonhoeffer, the German theologian whom James Cone also spoke of. Cone quotes Bonhoeffer as saying, "When Christ calls a man, he bids him come and die."[10] We wear these crosses around our necks, these symbols of an innocent man, lynched by the authorities because of pressure from a mob. Before we put them on, we should go cold with the fear that we would wear them under false pretenses, that we would bear false witness to who Jesus was, to what Jesus did.

I cannot tell you what to do about this truth of our history and our present. What I can tell you is that the next to the last commandment forbids us from bearing false witness against our neighbors. I can tell you that hundreds if not thousands of KKK members rallied in the town of my birth, Charlottesville, Virginia, yesterday, and I was not there to stand against them. The poem "Christ Recrucified" by Countee Cullen sums up the theology Cone is trying to share:

> The South is crucifying Christ again
> By all the laws of ancient rite and rule:
> The ribald cries of "Save Yourself" and "Fool"
> Din in his ears, the thorns grope for his brain,
> And where they bit, swift springing rivers stain
> His gaudy, purple robe of ridicule
> With sullen red; and acid wine to cool
> His thirst is thrust at him, with lurking pain.
> Christ's awful wrong is that he's dark of hue,
> The sin for which no blamelessness atones;
> But lest the sameness of the cross should tire
> They kill him now with famished tongues of fire,
> And while he burns, good men, and women, too,
> Shout, battling for his black and brittle bones.[11]

We are not guilty of the sin of murder. We did not do this killing. We did not ask for it. We were not consulted. But we let it stand. And we ignore its systemic nature. And we ignore its lessons. And we have stayed silent. We have borne false witness, and we have the chance today to turn aside from that sin, to lay it down, and to move forward with a scathing commitment to truth. And, incidentally, to also be ready to tell even our very best friend, "Honestly, those pants would probably look better on a cow than they do on you."

Notes

1. Langston Hughes, with David Roessel, ed., *Langston Hughes Poems* (New York: Everyman's Library, 1999) 119.

2. James H. Cone, *The Cross and the Lynching Tree* (Maryknoll NY: Orbis Books, 2011) 400, Kindle Edition.

3. Ibid., 354–430.

4. Ibid., 1477.

5. Ibid., 678.

6. Ibid., 2121.

7. "Shots Fired, Pt. 1," aired 17 March 2017, www.radiolab.org/story/shots-fired-part-1/.

8. Ibid.

9. Circles of Hope are groups made up of members from St. John's and Providence Baptist (predominantly white churches) and members from Friendship Missionary Baptist (a predominantly black church). The groups were started in response to the events of September 2016 in Charlotte, when protests turned violent after the police shooting of Keith Lamont Scott. They were started in cooperation between these three churches, with participants from each church in each group.

10. Cone, *The Cross and the Lynching Tree*, 2195.

11. Quoted in Cone, *The Cross and the Lynching Tree*, 2779.

Waking Up

A Challenge for White People

You know that feeling you have on a Sunday afternoon, say late fall or early winter, when you've fallen asleep on your couch and sleep really hard—harder than you meant to—and you wake up feeling heavy and groggy and unsure of where you are or what your name is? Waking up to my privilege, my responsibility, and my role in racial justice has been something like that for me. There's been quite a few questions popping around in my brain. "What did I do? What did I say? Why is that wrong? What should I be doing?" I'll tell you one thing I've learned for sure: my personal work is with white people. I have heard many white people saying, "What about black people? What is their responsibility? What about that horrible hip-hop? What about all the crime in their neighborhoods?" I have heard the dismay in the voices of those who have made what they believed to be genuine efforts at reconciliation, both black and white, as they came up against what felt like the futility of those efforts. It comes down to something as basic as the rules of bullying.

Do you know how to pick a bully out of the crowd? Here are the telltale signs:

1. The bully has the loudest voice.
2. The bully is not listening to any voice but their own. They talk over everyone else.

3. The bully has an excuse for everything they're accused of or confronted with but accepts no excuses of any kind from anyone else.

4. The bully will use any means necessary to keep what they have or to get what they want.

5. The bully never stops these behaviors until someone forces them to stop.

The bad news for white people is this: we are the bullies.

I know white people well, being one of them. There are several things we don't like:

• Speeding tickets (or any involvement with authority figures that cramps our style)
• People who talk during movies
• People who belong to the other political party
• People who don't pull their weight in group projects
• Black Entertainment Television

But really, the thing white people hate the worst is being treated as one entity—few people do. I could bet good money that I will get multiple emails or messages from individual white people who love BET or talking during movies or working in groups and that I shouldn't generalize. They will not recognize that being an individual has been a significant part of their privilege. And, not having been the stereotypical "bully" who, as we all know, is only interested in other kids' lunch money, white people will hate to own the idea that we are bullies.

I have been in innumerable conversations with white people during which they delineate a person in their narrative as "black." "My friend, Mary, who's black . . ." or "Gary, the black guy down at the station," or whatever. The privilege of white people is that we are individuals—we have a full, individualized, specialized, applies-only-to-us personhood. A black person, no matter how wonderful, always belongs to a group. A smart black student. A nice black lady. A good black doctor. It is important to note that few of the white people with whom I have been in contact over the years were overtly racist or hateful. Most would identify themselves as not racist in any way, shape, or color-differentiating process. But this is where we've ignored the subtle genius of privilege—we don't see what we don't have to see. We can live in protected, even gated neighborhoods; we can raise our children away from those we don't want to be with, including people who are overtly racist; we have absolute freedom of movement and, with that, the ability to stay willfully ignorant of what is going on with our brothers and sisters of color.

That willful part is important to acknowledge. It's not like our black brothers and sisters have not been telling us what is going on. What is rap and hip-hop culture if not an effort to share some horrible truths? Have we not read Toni Morrison? Maya Angelou? Richard Wright? Ralph Ellison? James Baldwin? Angie Thomas? Cornel West? Have we not heard, again and again, what is happening in urban schools? Story after story after story after story. And white people have clung with everything we had to the lie of "bootstrap" economics: that the reason a person, any person, is in poverty is that they did not work hard enough or were not smart enough or didn't take enough advantage of the opportunities given to them. We used successful black people against those who could not achieve success. *This black family raised fourteen children, and all of them became doctors or lawyers. What's wrong with the rest of you?* I've seen the confusion on people's faces and I've heard the anger and disappointment in their voices. "We've done everything we can," we say as we get back in our minivans to return to our white neighborhoods. "The rest is up to them."

Embracing Our Guilt

Another thing white people (and all bullies everywhere) hate is being made to feel guilty. Guilt gets a bad rap. I don't advocate that we return to a theology that is *all* about guilt—we shouldn't have to live in a faith that only speaks to us of our guilt. But guilt, like pain, has a reason. Pain lets us know that something is wrong. It says, "Hey! You should look at your leg! Something bit you!" Guilt serves a similar purpose. Like pain, it is not something to wallow in or hold on to. It is a warning signal in search of a solution. The reason that white people feel such guilt about black people in America is that we have never apologized for what we, together, did. It is an open wound that we have allowed to fester. We feel ashamed and saddened, but we haven't done the thing that leads to healing: offered acknowledgment along with genuine, remorseful penitence.

Because we did not individually own slaves, enact Jim Crow laws, or redline communities, we do not see ourselves has having done wrong. Yet, we know we are privileged—we know that resources are disproportionately divvied up to us. We feel a guilt we do not understand because we do not have to acknowledge that we are part of the systems—that we are the owners of those systems—that those systems are rigged to our benefit. So our conscience gnaws at us. It burns behind our eyes, making us angry at the reminders of it.

Have you ever been to Germany? Everyone should go. All across Germany, there are memorials—big ones and small ones—to those killed in the Holocaust. In Berlin, large areas of land are devoted to memorials, right in the center of town, right next to the government buildings. The Dachau concentration camp has been made into a museum. When we traveled to Germany as a family, my husband and children and I all went to Dachau with my husband's cousin, Christie, and her husband, Axel, who is German. Axel told me that Dachau feels to him like sacred ground. He was not even born when Nazis were committing the atrocities, but he had a profound sense of sorrow that his people had committed such horrible crimes. Axel did not spend every day in guilt or sorrow—he was a happy guy who ran a sheep farm and could flip a sheep on its tail to treat its hooves in one smooth motion. But he accepted his part of being a German and acknowledged the legacy of Nazism. He repented, along with his people, for crimes committed by his people. And the healing power of that remorse has allowed the German people to move forward and to become a force for good on the planet.

We have not done that work in the United States. Not yet. We have made no public apology for enslaving people. We have made no public apology for having laws that treated them as less than human or as less than complete humans. We have not made a single concession except to say, "Well, we stopped doing some stuff—that should be enough for you."

All white people bear responsibility for things from which we still gain advantages over others. We have separated ourselves from our black neighbors and excused ourselves for doing so. We have run them out of their neighborhoods with gentrification or to make way for the new bypass; we have reaped the benefit of laws that gave us enormous advantages of property and access to wealth; we have been okay with different standards being used against them by our public officials; we have ignored the overwhelming evidence that standardized tests are biased for white children and against black children. *We are still doing all of these things.*

So what are people of faith to do? We have absolutely no theological leg to stand on. There is no out from Jesus, who died so that those he loved could hear truth from his lips. There is no out from God's law, which requires that the single and only criterion for equality under the law and for the rights and privileges of complete citizenship is that they live in your village/town/city. If anything, people who have come from somewhere outside[1] are entitled, by the laws of the Old Testament and the New, to be protected, cared for, fed, housed, and treated kindly, with the same love a person shows himself or herself.

We have broken this law. We have broken the commandment not to bear false witness against our neighbor with our willful ignorance and our silence. We know this already. In our hearts we know our sin in this area, and that is why the guilt is so unbearable. Our anger at anyone pointing out these sins to us; our anger—which is another blight on our society, which stops the conversation and any possibility of moving forward—is directly related to our guilt. We choose not to see that owning that guilt collectively and offering both repentance and reparation for the harm we have done might ease both our guilt and our anger as it offers justice to those we have oppressed.

Our path to healing is like that old bear hunt game we played as kids: we can't go around the lake, can't go over it, can't go under it—we have to go through it.

Fortunately for us, our faith offers us a way of redemption:

1. Confess our sins. Openly. Publicly. Honestly. Completely. Wholeheartedly. Without conditions or exceptions.

2. Ask forgiveness—from God and from our brothers and sisters of color. No amount of "good work" or "not being racist" excuses us from this.

3. Stop doing the same *skubalon*² immediately. This will mean addressing discriminating practices in our workplaces, in our cities, in our schools, and in our neighborhoods. It will mean more listening than talking.

4. Make amends. Speak openly about our mistakes and about our remorse. Encourage others to do the same.

5. Accept God's forgiveness and move forward. It is not the job of the black community to make us feel okay. It is their right to forgive or not to forgive as their hearts lead them. Ours is the next move, and it is to build back the trust we have broken again and again. They will know we are sorry by our love, by our love . . . .

Before you decide what you will do about this racial divide (and rest assured that *you will do something*—doing nothing *is* doing something), think about this: what is holding you back? Are you worried that someone is going to get away with something? That somebody will get something he didn't work for, or somebody will get something for free that you had to work for? The first step is to start acknowledging that we all have things we didn't work for—white people have generations of inherited wealth denied to those we have oppressed, along with good-old-boy systems and countless gimmes offered to us throughout our lives. There are many good resources available to help in this process.³ If we can acknowledge that we didn't earn everything we have, then we can get started on the work of allowing others to experience that grace as well. I love to have conversations with business people (or other professional people like lawyers and doctors) about my salary as a minister. They know they make more money than I do—sometimes by several exponential factors. They know I have a lot of education. They know I work hard. And so they say to me, "You chose the wrong profession," as if I should have neglected my call to ministry or to teaching, ignored my gifts and talents, and become the world's worst hedge fund manager because at least then I could make more money. By the same token, I make more money, by exponential factors, than the hard-working people who clean the building in which I work. If this were a true meritocracy, their work would be valued as much as mine, and my work would be valued as much as that of some financial whiz. Privilege is not fair, and we all live with it all the time.

Are you worried that people will be angry with you? That people will not like you if you stand up for the rights of your black brothers and sisters? I can ease your mind about that right now: People will absolutely be angry with you, and some of them will not like you if you stand up for the rights of your black brothers and sisters. But, unless I miss my guess, you are not in middle school. If Christians, individually and corporately, are not strong enough to stand up to some petulant anger and to deal with people not liking us, then Christianity is truly dead and Jesus is slamming his head against the walls of heaven. Joan of Arc got burned at the stake, as did Girolamo Savonarola and William Tyndale; Christians have been beaten, imprisoned, tortured, killed, eaten by lions, and had poop thrown at them since day one. Why do modern Christians expect that nothing will be required of us except periodically showing up on Sundays and taking a few teenagers on mission trips?[4] There is a joy in bravery and camaraderie in doing courageous acts with other people. One of the few things that is forbidden to us as people of faith is fear. We must earn respect, and when others see you standing up for the rights of people, especially if you risk something in order to do so, they will give you their respect. Anything is better than continuing to be the silent mash of white bread—tasteless, gummy, and utterly without salt or flavor—that the white community has become.

I wish I had better news. I wish I could tell you that it is all behind us and that all we have to do is put it to bed. But that is not the case. And you know that it is not the case. I cannot tell you what part is yours to do. I can tell you that there is something to do in every facet of life: there is work for bankers and financial planners and accountants and employees of the IRS; there is work for police officers and administrators, for lawyers and judges, and legislators and (God help us) other politicians; there is work for developers and home builders and city planners and investors; there is work for teachers and doctors and pin-cushion manufacturers and builders of robots and owners of fast-food restaurants and managers of big-box stores and sit-com writers. There is great work for ministers, who could be preaching regularly about the call of biblical hospitality, who could be modeling courage for their people, who could be introducing ways for people to show their remorse and gain forgiveness. Whoever you are, whatever you do for a living or for your vocation, there is work that you can be doing toward true racial reconciliation.

Notes

1. That would include people whom our ancestors kidnapped and enslaved and brought here forcibly, as well as all their progeny.

2. The Apostle Paul uses this slang word in Scripture (Phil 3:8)—see www.blueletterbible.org/lang/lexicon/lexicon.cfm?Strongs=G4657&t=NIV. If he can use it, so can I.

3. See the Privilege Walk Activity at www.albany.edu/ssw/efc/pdf/Module%205_1_Privilege%20Walk%20Activity.pdf. It is a simple example of a privilege walk. Here is another activity: www.kosmosjournal.org/news/generation-waking-up-privilege-and-social-identity-getting-real/. Additional sources are listed at the end of this book.

4. Despite the inconvenience of sleeping on a leaking air mattress in a church Sunday school room for a week, this last one does *not* count as torture.

11

Apply Good Theology to Wound; Repeat as Necessary

If you would like to be part of the healing process[1] that this nation (and all others) will have to go through, here are some possible ways forward.

1. *Lead.* If you are in leadership in your community of faith, the first thing for you to do is your own work. We cannot progress anywhere on an issue as difficult as racial reconciliation without doing hard work within ourselves. Leaders in this process cannot be insecure. Jesus, you might notice, has little tolerance for the insecurities of his followers; he tends to focus on the fact that we should know who we are and whose we are and let everything else go (including other people's ideas of who we should be). Get training, have dialogs with each other, and listen and pay attention to what the black people in your community are saying. Know why you are doing what you do. At the end of this book, you will find a section on the resources already available—use them; do your homework. Rosa Parks did not just show up one day on a bus, too tired to get up and move. She had training. She planned to do what she did. She knew what she was going to do, she knew why she was doing it, and she knew what the consequences would be. You may not be called to civil disobedience, but you are certainly going to encounter pushback. Be responsible—prepare yourself and try not to be naïve about what you are doing.

2. *Buy in.* Bring other people along with you. If you are the pastor of a church, it is important to remember that you represent your congregation. You are the symbol of that particular church or community of faith; you are not an individual acting on your own. Once you have trained yourself, you need to work with your community and bring some of them with you in the work of racial reconciliation. Before you can do any significant work, you need to have the leadership of your community standing with you. Not having the buy-in of your community is a great way to split a community of faith in two. Share with your leadership where you are and what you would like to do. Share what it means to you and what your theological backing is for the work. Offer training for your leadership, and, before you step into any civil rights activities outside of your own community of faith, make sure that they know what you are doing, why you are doing it, and have bought into it by either blessing your participation without them or participating with you.

If you are not the pastor but have another staff role or have some position of leadership, you will need the buy-in of the main leader. If the head of your organization has not bought into this work, then the organization has not bought into it, and so no one in the organization can do the work.[2] You can defy this rule and split your community, or you can leave the organization. But if you stay, unless the head of the organization buys into your significant, culture-changing work, the work will not succeed.

Understand that the person with the greatest privilege in the community of faith system is the pastor (or priest or rector or rabbi or imam). This person has the attention and trust of the entire community. This person must understand his or her own privilege in the system in order for the work of racial reconciliation to begin. The work of the leader of an organization always affects the system. Leaders bring the system with them—or leave it behind. Systems that are able to do culture-changing work are those that understand how the leader/community relationship works. They do not allow their leader to offer false humility (as in, "You guys can make that decision without me! I will do whatever you say!"), nor do they allow their leader to move forward without them (as in "I am doing this whether you guys like it or not!"). Being part of a community of faith means that we are inextricably tied together. Any progress we make going down the road, we make together. If your pastor/rector/rabbi/imam/priest does not know this, the time to teach them is right now.

3. *Prioritize.* In the past, the church and many communities of faith have prioritized a great many things over hospitality: morality (as *they* set it), fitting in, building programs, citizenship, and even "hard work," despite the careful ways in which the Apostle Paul espouses a theology of grace. There is ample evidence in the Bible (and, again, in the lived-out practice of being people of faith) to justify applying the biblical principles of hospitality first and worrying about everything else later on. In the church I served from 2001–2018, the covenant calls for us to worship together, to build community together, to share our resources (including our money and our time), to do our own spiritual work apart from the church, and to do servant ministry in the world. As part of our covenant, we promise to "admonish each other as occasion may require."

Notice that this admonishment is done *inside* community. Some of you may be horribly uncomfortable about letting someone into community with you before they have straightened up their behavior. Unfortunately, biblical hospitality offers no caveats for behavior or anything else. Hospitality comes first, including providing safety, welcome, kindness, care, and, yes, even love. Inside community, we have space to help each other keep from hurting ourselves or others, but that comes after we are included in community. We are ill-equipped to judge each other. Only after we have bound ourselves inextricably to each other—standing at birthing beds and death beds, helping each other raise our children, walking with each other through thick and thin—do we earn the right to speak to each other about our behaviors. Billie Holiday said, "You've got to have something to eat and a little love in your life before you can hold still for any damn body's sermon on how to behave."[3] If communities of faith began to prioritize the task of offering hospitality to people over property, over morality, over everything else, we would look very different in the world.

4. *Support.* Support each other inside your own community. Support others in the larger community. Reach out for help from people who are safe for you. Make your mantra "No one does this work alone. No one does this work alone. NO ONE does this work alone. No one DOES this work alone. No one does THIS WORK alone. No one does this work ALONE."

My friend, Janet, led our Bible study recently and shared a passage from the November 17 entry in the excellent resource, *Common Prayer: A Liturgy for Ordinary Radicals.* The entry for that day offers a quote from Ronald Rolheiser, president of the Oblate School of Theology in San Antonio, Texas:

> If the Catholicism that I was raised in had a fault, and it did, it was precisely that it did not allow for mistakes. It demanded that you get it right the first time. There was supposed to be no need for a second chance. If you made a mistake, you lived with it and, like the rich young man, were doomed to be sad, at least for the rest of your life. A serious mistake was a permanent stigmatization, a mark that you wore like Cain. . . . We need a theology of brokenness. We need a theology which teaches us that even though we cannot unscramble an egg, God's grace lets us live happily and with renewed innocence far beyond any egg we may have scrambled. We need a theology that teaches us that God does not just give us one chance, but that every time we close a door, he opens another one for us.[4]

As always, our pathway forward is through the acknowledgment that we have sinned, the apology for doing so, and the acceptance of forgiveness and grace. Our theology must offer us space in which to seek our own peace, our own responsibility, and move forward.

When I was in the doorway of the Omni Hotel garage in Charlotte, just after the police released the first round of tear gas, as the crowd pressed in together, unable to react or move, a young black woman close to me looked me in the eye and yelled, "White silence equals violence!" My first reaction was defensive. I was right there with her—the tear gas was getting in my eyes, too. What more was

I supposed to do? But I get it now. I was silent for a long, long time. I have been an adult for thirty years, and I am just now beginning, really, to talk about what I know is true regarding our treatment of our black brothers and sisters. And so I want to share this:

> Lord, let this be my prayer:
> that I learn to be quiet and listen to my brothers and sisters who need to be heard;
> that I learn to speak clearly, audibly, and with compassion to my brothers and sisters who need to listen;
> that I work first for the safety of my brothers and sisters and that I let the other stuff go;
> that I put people before property, before culture, before rules, before perception, and before personal comfort;
> that I put away my own insecurities and grow a thick skin, so I can do the work I am called to do;
> that I find the right words, so those who need to hear, can do so;
> and that I learn to see the shadow of the lynching tree in the cross, so I remember the One to whom I belong.
> Amen.

Notes

1. Personally, I do not see an "out" for any Christian that gives us permission not to do the work of radical inclusion. This would involve racial inclusion as well as the inclusion of everyone else we have ostracized, including our siblings in the LGBTQ and disabled communities.

2. This is not my rule. I did not make it up. It is observable fact.

3. Quoted in Stacy Holman Jones, *Torch Singing* (Plymouth UK: Altmira Press, 2007).

4. Quoted in Shane Claiborne, Jonathan Wilson-Hartgrove, Enuma Okoro, *Common Prayer: A Liturgy for Ordinary Radicals* (Grand Rapids MI: Zondervan, 2010) 523.

12

The Rewards: Grace and Joy

There is a joy in the journey
There's a light we can love on the way
There is a wonder and wildness to life
And freedom for those who obey
— Michael Card

Joy. I think often of a scene from a 1980s movie called *The Mission*. It starred Jeremy Irons as a Catholic priest named Father Gabriel, called to the wilderness of South America, and Robert DeNiro as Rodrigo Mendoza, the former owner of a slave ship who submits himself to penance under this priest. There is a powerful scene during which Father Gabriel is leading Mendoza through the rain forest, back to a mission where he will serve the native people he has been enslaving. The movie doesn't say who ordained that Mendoza carry all of his armor and weaponry through the jungle although it's implied that Mendoza laid this burden on himself. At one point, the group must climb out of a river, up the side of a ravine. Mendoza struggles, caught on the rocks, the impossibly heavy weight of his former life pulling him back. Father Gabriel takes a machete, leans over, hacks through the rope between Mendoza and his net full of rusted, dirty armor, and it falls back into the river, freeing Mendoza to complete the climb.

There are no words in this scene. Nothing is said. But Mendoza collapses in tears as the weight of his sins falls from him. And he climbs into a new life. That is the reward of the work of racial reconciliation.

I felt it on a summer evening in St. Louis, Missouri, at a Steak & Shake, still electrified by the events of the day, of standing for justice and being arrested for doing so. I have read it in the words of the people of my church who participated with me in some difficult conversations during my doctoral project. We could watch each other's eyes being opened—sometimes a physical, wide-eyed stare—when we allowed ourselves to truly listen to the words of our black brothers and sisters. White people have no idea of the burden we carry every day, the weight of the thing we pretend not to notice. We joke about it, dance around it, ignore it, and get angry when anyone else draws attention to it. Some of the angriest people in the planet are those with the most privilege, carrying that bag of anger in their cars and inside stores and to their workplaces and into their living room chairs.

As Michael Card so beautifully sings, "There is a joy in the journey/There's a light we can love on the way." I have a friend named Joy. She is a member of the generation we call "The Silent Generation," those strong individuals who were children during the Depression and World War II, who came of age in the middle of the twentieth century. Her story, told with her permission, is that the culture in which she grew up was marked by significant racism, and her home, while not angrily or violently racist, was affected by that culture. As a young person, her nature hit against that racism and could not find a place for it. She did not feel it herself, and she didn't understand its nature.

She later became a teacher, taught high school math, and made friends with other teachers and professionals, black and white. In the last year, she has submitted herself to the difficult work of racial reconciliation, participating in multiple public and private conversations in which she has practiced fierce and powerful listening. She has been confessional about her journey. And, as she continues, joining with her "Circle of Hope" group (one of the groups with white and black members from St. John's and Friendship Missionary Baptist in Charlotte) to keep up the conversation, the joy she feels at bringing new friends into her circle, of understanding their stories and believing them, is all over her face. She does not have to apologize for the racism she witnessed when she was young; that is not hers to carry. She lays down only what armor she picked up. But, oh—the look on her face when she talks about her friends from Friendship Missionary Baptist.

At one meeting I was sitting behind her, and she was sitting next to a woman from Friendship. They were both former schoolteachers, about the same age. They bonded quickly. Had the planet, in that moment, handed them the reins to solve the world's problems, they could have taken care of them in the work of about an hour. That is the joy in the journey. We understand each other. We become more than we were. It is out there for you as well. Perhaps you have already had enough experience to tell you that it is possible, that you can be touched by this kind of joy. If so, then you know that it does not come cheaply; it is purchased with belief and trust and kindness and protection and respect and remorse and, yes, genuine love. I wish you well. I continue on this journey, too, with much work before me. But I believe in the banquet, and I believe the banquet is happening right now—and that we are all invited. There is plenty of food. It is being offered in an enormous room—at one of those expandable tables, perhaps from Ikea—and there is always room for one more.

Resources for Further Training

The Baptist Peace Fellowship of North American/ Bautistas por la Paz

300 Hawthorne Lane
Charlotte, NC 28204
www.bpfna.org

"Do Not Be Afraid" Training
Conflict Transformation Training:
www.bpfna.org/equip/conflict-transformation-training

Fellowship of Reconciliation

521 North Broadway
Nyack, NY 10960
www.forusa.org
Visit their bookstore: www.forusa.org/store.php

Mecklenburg Ministries

PO Box 11243
Charlotte NC 28220
www.meckmin.org
Soul to Soul, training led by Anne Van Newkirk

History South—Dr. Tom Hanchett

"Salad Bowl Suburbs"
www.historysouth.org/saladbowlintro/

Civil Conversations Project

www.civilconversationsproject.org
Their tag line is "Speaking together differently in order to live
together differently."

The Police Executive Research Forum

See "The Guiding Principles on Use of Force," 2016, www.police-
forum.org/assets/guidingprinciples1.pdf and "Advice from Police
Chiefs and Community Leaders on Building Trust," 2016, www.
policeforum.org/assets/policecommunitytrust.pdf.

Charlottesville Clergy Collective

Interfaith Unity Service (August 9, 2018)
www.cvilleclergycollective.org

Bibliography

Broach, Claude. "Bring Up Samuel." Sermon delivered at St. John's Baptist Church in Charlotte, NC, 30 June 1974.

Card, Michael. "Joy in the Journey." *The Final Word* (album). Sparrow Records. March 1987.

Chamblee, Katherine. "Progressing Backward: The Re-Opening of *Swann v. Charlotte-Mecklenburg Schools*," Swarthmore College, www.swarthmore.edu/writing/progressing-backward-re-opening-swann-v-charlotte-mecklenburg-schools (accessed 23 January 2017).

Claiborne, Shane, Jonathan Wilson-Hartgrove, Enuma Okoro. *Common Prayer: A Liturgy for Ordinary Radicals*. Grand Rapids MI: Zondervan, 2010.

"Coming to Ferguson." Training. Fellowship of Reconciliation and Black Lives Matter Movement of Ferguson MO. 2015.

Cone, James. *Martina & Malcolm & America: A Dream or a Nightmare*. New York: Maryknoll, 1991.

Cone, James. *The Cross and the Lynching Tree*. New York: Orbis Books, Kindle Edition, 2011.

"Do Not Be Afraid." Training. Baptist Peace Fellowship of North America/Bautistas Por La Paz. Kadia Edwards and LeDayne Polaski, facilitators. 2016.

Hanchett, Tom. "Melting Pot to Salad Bowl: Race in Charlotte Neighborhoods." Lecture. St. John's Baptist Church, Charlotte NC. 17 May 2016.

"Hope Chapel" File. From St. John's Baptist Church. Accessed October 2017.

Hughes, Langston. *Langston Hughes Poems.* Edited by David Roessel. New York: Everyman's Library, 1999.

Jones, Stacy Holman. *Torch Singing.* Plymouth UK: Altmira Press, 2007.

Miller, Arthur. *Death of a Salesman.* New York: Penguin Books, 1976.

Oden, Amy, editor. *And You Welcomed Me: A Sourcebook on Hospitality in Early Christianity.* Nashville: Abingdon Press, 2001.

"Privilege and Social Identity." www.kosmosjournal.org/news/generation-waking-up-privilege-and-social-identity-getting-real/.

"Privilege Walk." www.albany.edu/ssw/efc/pdf/Module%205_1_Privilege%20Walk%20Activity.pdf.

Rodgers, Richard and Oscar Hammerstein II. "You've Got to Be Carefully Taught." *South Pacific.* 1949.

"Shots Fired, Part I." Aired 17 March 2017. www.radiolab.org/story/shots-fired-part-1/.

"Souls of White Folks." Training. Mecklenburg Ministries. Anne Van Newkirk, facilitator. 2010.

Sutherland, Arthur. *I Was a Stranger: A Christian Theology of Hospitality.* Nashville: Abingdon Press, 2006.

Terry, Marshall, and Michael Tomsic. "New Research Shows Mecklenburg County among Worst for Economic Mobility." 6 May 2015. wfae.org/post/new-research-shows-mecklenburg-county-among-worst-economic-mobility. Accessed 23 January 2017.

Tillman, William, Rodney Taylor, and Lauren Brewer, editors. *Both-And: A Maston Reader.* T. B. Maston Foundation for Christian Ethics, 2011.

www.ingramcontent.com/pod-product-compliance
Lightning Source LLC
LaVergne TN
LVHW051746080426
835511LV00018B/3241